soul
happiness

soul
happiness

The 11 Secrets of Living with Purpose

Marnie McDermott

gladileen
MEDIA

To my Mac, for loving me.

contents

To Begin   xiii

    A word about bliss   xiv

    Soul happiness and me   xv

    The two Soul truths   xvi

    Using this book   xvii

    The power of simplicity   xix

    Soul happiness is already yours   xxii

PART ONE

Sync With Your Soul   1

CHAPTER 1

Secret 1: Happiness Is Your Right   3

    Happiness is now   4

    Recognise soul sadness   6

    Crave meaning   8

    The music of your Soul   9

CHAPTER 2

Secret 2: The Soul's Natural Order   15

    The Soul's code   17

    Destiny or decision   18

    The multiplicity of purpose   20

    Soul path and purpose   27

CHAPTER 3

Secret 3: Lessons Have Purpose 31

    Soul cycles of learning 34

    The 12 Soul lessons 36

    Recognise course corrections 38

    Release false truths 39

CHAPTER 4

Secret 4: Truth Lives In Your Heart 47

    Be self-full 49

    Trust your true north 51

    Give yourself permission to feel 52

    Let your values guide you 54

CHAPTER 5

Secret 5: Gifts Are For Sharing 63

    Look within 65

    Believe you are special 67

    Be multi-passionate 68

    Do what you love today 70

    The 12 Soul gifts 71

CHAPTER 6

Secret 6: You Are The Path 81

    You already know 84

    The first true you 85

    The secrets of the stars 88

    Signs and synchronicities 95

PART TWO
Be In Soul Flow   101

CHAPTER 7
Secret 7: Say Yes To Your Soul   103
    The secret of purpose   105
    Your Soul map   107
    Purpose is what's true for you   116

CHAPTER 8
Secret 8: Create Your Reality   125
    Creation follows intention   127
    The art of intention   129
    Soulful goals   131
    Your time is now   134
    Infuse your life with purpose   135

CHAPTER 9
Secret 9: Manifest Your Dreams   145
    You can manifest whatever you want   148
    We live in a material world for a reason   149
    What you receive is based on what you believe   151
    The biggest block is your inner balance   152
    The art of manifesting   153
    The ultimate manifestation secret   156

CHAPTER 10

Secret 10: Be Authentically You   161

    The power of authenticity   164

    Signs you are suppressing your authentic self   165

    Claim Your Soul Power   167

    The keys to living authentically   169

CHAPTER 11

Secret 11: Grow Some More   175

    The anatomy of change   177

    The principles of Soul growth   181

    Let your intuition be your guide   188

    Respond to every call that excites your spirit   189

To End   195

11 Simple Promises   197

Glossary Of Terms   199

The Trinity Of Soul Happiness   200

About The Author   202

to begin

Truth is not something outside to be discovered,
it is something inside to be realised.
~ OSHO

Your happiness is intrinsically linked with your life purpose. There's a connection, a parallel, an undeniable correlation between the two. So, as much as this is a book about happiness, it is also a book about purpose.

The deepest happiness – what I call 'enduring bliss' – is yours when you live your life in harmony with your Soul purpose. To be in harmony with your Soul purpose, you must also be in harmony with your true self. It is impossible to do one without the other.

Soul happiness is what you experience when your life is in sync with both your true purpose and your authentic self. When you live in this way, you have access to all the beauty, abundance and love your heart desires.

I introduced the concept of Soul happiness in the first book in this series, *Beyond Happiness: The 12 Principles of Enduring Bliss.* In it, I described Soul happiness as the only truly enduring state of happiness we can experience in our lives. *Beyond Happiness* was about the essential foundations of enduring bliss and the tools to balance every part of you – mind, body, emotion and spirit.

This book is the next stage of the journey. *Soul Happiness* guides you to embrace the power and purpose that lies within you. To embody your authentic essence and align with your truth.

Ultimately, it shows you how to live the life you are destined to live.

A word about bliss

Let's consider happiness.

We are all happy. To some degree. Yet many of us settle for what I call 'fleeting happiness'. In *Beyond Happiness*, I explain how the four happiness traps – storybook happiness, surprise happiness, surrogate happiness and someday happiness – all result in fleeting happiness. It's the sort of happiness that comes from what you have and what you do, rather than the happiness that comes from who you are.

Fleeting happiness is exactly that. It comes and it goes. And we spend most of our lives desperately looking for it, pursuing it, and even trying to create it. Happiness of the mind is when we believe happiness resides outside us.

We can settle for fleeting happiness without realising we have the power to move beyond it.

Happiness transforms from fleeting to enduring the moment you really embrace and love the brilliance of you. Enduring bliss, or lifelong happiness comes from happiness of the Soul rather than happiness of the mind.

Let me explain further.

Happiness of the mind is doing things you think you have to do to be happy. Happiness of the Soul is finding purpose, joy and abundance in doing what you love.

Happiness of the mind is about seeking, striving, pursuing and always having to do more. Happiness of the Soul is the peaceful contentment of being truly you.

Happiness of the mind is focusing on the love around us. Happiness of the Soul is focusing on the love within us. In fact, it's when we *become* love and when we *become* happiness.

Soul happiness and me

If you have read *Beyond Happiness*, you will be familiar with some of the most significant circumstances and moments in my life that profoundly shaped who I was and how I viewed my world. I will share more with you through this book.

Amazing things began happening in my life when I started to make the smallest changes. Changes like actually taking notice of the body I was in, and choosing to embrace, love and nourish it. Like deciding to let go of a big ball of bundled up hurts. And like starting to make time for me in my day, in stillness and silence.

All these seemingly unconnected things were actually very much connected. I didn't realise it at the time, but I was rebalancing every part of myself. My mind. My body. My emotions. And my spirit. What I was really doing was creating space in my life for me. Until that point, my life had been shaped by my perception of who and what I believed others wanted me to be. Until that point, my focus in life was permanently outward. Full of distraction and drama and doing so many things I didn't really want to be doing! But once I followed the steps I outlined in *Beyond Happiness*, my life started to transform. Mostly because I started creating the space for me in my life.

It was like a system reboot, a return to factory settings. That new space was waiting to be filled with something awe-inspiring. When I created the space for me, I also created the space for inner conversations about dreams, and love, and intention, and living in a way that honoured who I was. And that's when the voice of Purpose started quietly guiding me deeper within to become who I was always meant to be. I created the space for Soul happiness.

Through the process of writing this book, I have been drawn to early memories of writing, creating and inspiring others. The truth is, on some level of my being, I have always known who I am and what I am here to do. But sometimes it can feel overwhelming – truly astonishingly humbling – when you look yourself in the heart and see the power of your Soul.

And I've realised that even when we think we know our purpose, we've really only glimpsed a part of it. I discovered that we have to move forward – sometimes blindly, with only trust, faith and belief to guide us – in order for the next step on our path to be revealed.

If we knew the full scale of our journey at the beginning, so many of us would be too scared to take the first step. And that is why, even now, the stepping stones on my path reveal themselves gradually. Piece by piece, one bite-sized chunk at a time. And it will be the same for you too.

It's like a kind of grown-up version of a star chart – you know, the kind that hung on your fridge as a kid to motivate you to do your household chores. The steps toward your purpose are stars. And you need to complete each one – step by step, star by star – until eventually you fill the chart. As a kid, it was a daunting task to consider. But if we stuck it out, soon enough, there was a shiny golden trail showing how far we'd come.

I've discovered it's no different with purpose. With each step you become a bigger, brighter more radiant version of yourself. The wider and deeper you go, the more you realise that purpose is not about what you do. It is about who you are. And with each step you move closer to your own Soul.

That's what this book will show you. That's where we're headed.

The two Soul truths

There's an old adage about the only certainties in life being death and taxes.

That may be true of a physical existence. But of a Soulful existence there are two further certainties.

The first is that every single one of us has a unique and very special reason for being here. It's called purpose. And, for most of us, it is the one thing that causes the most confusion, anxiety and even despair in our lives. The mere thought leaves us sighing deeply and puzzling over and over again, *what is my purpose?*

The second is that we have already set the intention for how we will fulfil that purpose. This is true no matter what path we decide to take to get there. There may be many roads to choose from, but eventually each and every one will lead you exactly where you intended to go. Some paths may be simple, quick and easy. Others will be more challenging and take longer. But eventually, we always get where we need to be. There's the long way and there's the short way. Either way, you are always on the right track.

So often when people talk about life purpose, they think only in terms of their outer actions, success and achievement. The truth is, Soul purpose is so much more encompassing than just what you do. Soul purpose is not about your job, or what you have, or what you create. Soul purpose is all about who you are. It is about you at the deepest level. You must fulfil your inner purpose, before you can harness your true talents and gifts and make a difference for others. That is why this book has a focus on inner purpose as the path to outer purpose.

Using this book

This book is about helping you to get back in sync with your Soul and by doing so, to create a world of possibility, excitement, fulfilment, beauty, abundance and happiness in your life. Soul happiness comes naturally when we say yes to our Soul, our purpose, our true self, and our reason for being here right now.

My desire for every book I write is that it will be simple to understand and easy to apply. *Soul Happiness* is no different.

This book is about balancing the spiritual with the practical – we are sacred beings in earthly bodies. It is up to us to harness the logical, practical side of ourselves and to manifest our purpose in the here and now. To take it from what I call 'the dreaming' into 'the doing'.

To create anything in our life, first we must have the insight and the intention. In other words know who we are and what we want (the dreaming), before we can take the action, or the steps towards making it a reality (the doing).

This book is divided into two parts giving you the 11 Secrets of Living with Purpose.

In each part my intention is to answer the 'why?' by sharing knowledge, wisdom and inspiration, then to answer the 'how?' by giving you simple, practical tools and exercises. It's about harnessing your own inner knowing and using it to take inspired action.

Part 1: Sync With Your Soul

This part enables you to unlock your own Soul code for greater awareness of yourself and your Soul purpose. You will:

- Understand the link between happiness and purpose
- Learn about the Soul's nature and flow
- Discover the four aspects of Soul purpose
- Learn how to decipher your Soul challenges, Soul values, Soul character and Soul path.

Part 2: Be In Soul Flow

This part gives you the tools for living an authentic life, in tune with who you are and what you are here to do. You will:

- Learn how to create your own Soul map
- Discover the secrets of manifesting

- Master the four keys of authentic living
- Understand the principles of Soul growth.

Most chapters begin with a story from my own journey into Soul happiness and Soul purpose. They typically focus on life-changing moments of insight, lessons and discoveries. You know, those magical a-ha moments where light streams into your consciousness. Some are from decades ago; others are more recent. Each was carefully chosen to show the principles we'll be discussing in action.

Like *Beyond Happiness*, this book has been created as a programme. Each week, read a chapter, absorb it, reflect on it, and start working on it.

That being said, my natural instinct with books like this is to devour them from cover to cover. Then I sit with the new knowledge, and let the insights bubble up into awareness. Then I like to return for a second, more leisurely and even deeper read. That's my thing. You'll have yours. Just do what feels right for you. There is no right or wrong.

Start where you want. Take as long as you need. Absorb as much as you need. Trust you'll get where you need to go when the time is right.

The power of simplicity

I want to give you the insight, the inspiration and the ability to make changes in your life. So each chapter in this book also ends with some simple tools for you to put what you've learned into action. Although these tasks may challenge you, and require time and effort, they are not difficult.

Don't be fooled, however, by their simplicity. They are also deceptively powerful. If you make a promise to yourself that you will try them, you will see a difference in how you think and how you feel.

Simple reflection

Through this book, I aim to draw out your own inner wisdom. Each chapter includes a simple reflection exercise. This is about self-discovery and allowing yourself to grow. We always have the answers we need within us, though they often take time to present themselves. It is likely that the days and weeks after reading this book will bring you more insights than just those you receive while turning its pages. So allow yourself plenty of time for reflection.

Use a journal for this reflection. If you don't already have one, please get one. The design doesn't matter. Whether it's simple, elegant, funky, beautiful, or inspirational, the choice is yours. The most important thing is that you love it!

If you choose not to do the simple reflections, write in your journal anyway. I call my journal my 'bliss journal'. It's my trusted confidant and the keeper of my inner wisdom. Your bliss journal will become the keeper of your dreams and a place for you to share the voice of your heart. It doesn't matter what you write; just write freely and without censoring anything that comes to mind. Mornings are an amazing time for inspiration, and journaling is a wonderful way to access your inner wisdom.

You may also wish to use the Soul Happiness companion workbook, designed to be used side-by-side with this book, guiding you through your own reflections, discovery and a-ha moments. It is available from my website **www.marniemcdermott.com**

Simple promise

Affirmations have become a popular way of positively reframing our thoughts to focus on the things we desire. When you make an affirmation, you are making a statement about the way you would like something to be.

I take the idea of an affirmation further by encouraging you to make a simple promise to yourself. For your simple promises to be effective, say them as often as you can in your head, aloud, or even looking in the mirror. It doesn't matter how you do it. Perhaps even write them down, record them on your phone, or display them somewhere you can see them.

A promise combines the power and positive intention of an affirmation, with the commitment of a promise from the heart. When you make a promise to yourself, you acknowledge that you are worthy of receiving good things.

Simple practice

I believe in the power of just doing *something*. The moment you do something, you make a conscious change. Each chapter ends with some ideas for simple practices to try.

Simple practice brings your attention to specific actions you can take to experience the ideas discussed in the chapter. These may appear obvious, yet so often, even when we know what we need to do, we just don't take the steps and actually do it.

You don't have to do everything; just choose one thing. If something different comes to mind and resonates strongly for you, go with it!

Simple meditation

I have included several meditations in this book. They will guide you on an inner journey and create the space for deeper insights, awareness and connection.

Meditations are best when you close your eyes and listen to someone's voice. Record the meditations in this book for yourself, allowing silences where needed. You can also download the audio files of the meditations in this book from my website **www.marniemcdermott.com**

Remember, beautiful things grow from tiny seeds. Sometimes when we look back on our lives, we realise that the most simple changes or decisions created the most far-reaching ripples. Even choosing just one simple thing for yourself in each chapter will start a beautiful ripple in your life.

Soul happiness is already yours

Here's the thing, the ultimate secret I've discovered about Soul happiness: it's already yours.

Our Soul ensures we have everything we need for this lifetime. It's like you already have the secret file sitting on your desk. It contains all the plans, all the memos, and all the supporting information you need for your happiest life; one where you live with purpose.

You just need to open the file, read and study the contents and decide what you will do with the information.

As you work through this book, you may discover that what you are doing right now actually contains the seeds from which your true purpose will flourish.

Whether or not you are ready to see it for yourself, I believe the wisest part of you already knows three sacred truths – who you are, what you are here to learn, and how you will serve others. And the sooner you remember this, the more free you will be.

How will you know? Tune in to your 'goose bump' moments. They are the quiet whispers from your Soul letting you know you have connected with the light inside you. Take note. It's a sign from your Soul to look deeper.

Life calls us to dream and when we take action, our dreams come alive in ways we may never have imagined. Align your inner self with how you live your life and you will have Soul happiness.

Discovering your purpose comes down to discovering who you really are. This book is a step-by-step guide to living life in sync with your Soul.

Everything happens with divine perfection. The fact you are reading this book, right here, right now, is a perfect stepping stone, another golden star, on your path in this life.

Keep shining, beautiful you.

With love,

Marnie x

January 2014

PART ONE

sync with your soul

The moment you bring yourself back into alignment with

who you really are and what your purpose really is,

that's the moment you fill every part of your life with

the sweetness and beauty of your spirit.

The deepest questions require the deepest journeys. Allowing yourself the time for that inward journey – to just be at one with yourself, to feel a greater sense of awareness, to feel peace and love spread through your body – is not wasted time. Nothing about spending time with yourself is wasted.

Know that the answers to all your deepest questions about your life are closer than you think. Almost right under your nose. All the information you need has been programmed into your Soul code. Your Soul code isn't complicated, and doesn't require complex deciphering.

In fact, this part of the book will show you how simple and easy it is to decode. The chapters that follow are about inspiring you to see that your purpose in life is more about who you are than what you do. They show you how to recognise the lessons, values and gifts that are part of your Soul code, and they show you how to piece together the clues of the life you are destined to live.

Your true purpose in life lies not in an outward expression of brilliance; it lies in seeing the brilliance of your true self. These keys will guide you to a deeper connection with your Soul-self.

CHAPTER 1

secret 1: happiness is your right

Heaven on earth is a choice you must make, not a place you must find.
~ Wayne Dyer

When you claim happiness as your right, when you know happiness lies within you, you are better able to align your inner and outer worlds.

It's an interesting thing. It seems the more my inner self and my outer life align – the more in sync I am – the more inwardly fulfilled, and content and peaceful I feel, and the more outwardly focused, driven and passionate I become.

In my 'old' life I remember working so often, all the hours under the sun, for other people. To do what I felt I had to. Or in my leisure time doing what other people wanted to do. Frequently even saying what I thought other people wanted me to say. All this outer effort and over-focus was based on dizzying standards I had created for myself. And those standards were based on how I thought other people perceived me.

Every time I said yes to someone or something else, I really said no to my spirit. Many a time each 'Yes' would leave my breath caught in my heart. Yet another forced circumstance or reluctant responsibility based on what other people wanted me to do. My boss. My parents (bless them). Old loves. Old friends. And each time on a Soul level I believe I knew I wasn't honouring myself, but on a mental level I was too scared about what people would think of me to stand in my own power.

When we are too caught up in the illusions of our mind to hear the voice of our spirit, our feelings become our compass. Yet often our mind overrides our feelings. Our mind is our greatest creative power, a wonderful gift. Yet, full to the brim with beliefs, programmes, judgements and thoughts, it can also be our biggest handbrake.

My mind used to lead me. Urging me forward to bigger, better, more. Casually dismissing the breath caught in my heart, the growing feeling of emptiness and disconnection as nothing important. Easily fixed with yet another round of bigger, better, more.

Back then, the wheel of my life was totally out of balance and, believe me, the ride was bumpy. But the decision to start bringing myself back into balance created the space for me to say yes to me. In that space I felt free and happy. I consciously chose happiness as my right.

But that space allowed something else. It allowed me to connect to who I really am (inner purpose), and to understand what I am here to do (outer purpose).

What I'm saying is, although you will feel happier and more fulfilled and have more clarity when you are in balance, a life in balance is just the start. Really, there is a more important reason for being in balance, and that is to create the space for you to expand into an even more wondrous version of yourself. In that space you discover who you really are and hear the voice of purpose. And when you're living in complete harmony with who you are, magic happens. Deep Soul-filling joy happens. And, to me, that's Soul happiness. And that's your right.

Happiness is now

Happiness is not something outside of you that you need to chase or seek or pursue. It is not something that you earn nor is it a reward for success.

Happiness is within you. In every heartbeat. Always.

Happiness is not something that you finally reach at the end of your lifelong to-do list. It's not something that magically appears when your life is perfect.

Happiness is a choice. In every moment. A way of being.

And Soul happiness is who you are. Your divine self and your divine right. The natural state you were born to embody.

Your Soul is your source. Your essence, your being, your truth, your light, your power. It is Love. It is eternal. It is your home. It is not separate from you. Rather, you are intertwined together in oneness.

And that is why we are our happiest when we are our true, authentic selves. Being authentic means aligning our inner and outer selves; our inner and outer worlds.

Soul happiness is an encompassing philosophy of intertwined love, happiness and life purpose.

> *Soul happiness is a trinity within; I believe we can't truly be happy in a lifelong way unless we love ourselves, honour ourselves, and authentically live our Soul purpose. We are limiting happiness because we are limiting love. By loving yourself unconditionally, you give your true self a stage. When you love yourself, your spirit shines. You have purpose. You have peace of heart. You move from doing things you think you have to do to be happy, to finding joy and abundance in doing what you love. You change your vibration from one of seeking, striving, and pursuing to one of peaceful contentment. Happiness of the Soul is when we become love and when we become happiness. That is enduring bliss. Soul happiness transforms our daily experience of fleeting happiness into lifelong enduring bliss.*
>
> *~ Beyond Happiness: The 12 Principles of Enduring Bliss*

It's all within you. Right this very moment. Pure, unadulterated potential for bliss.

Recognise soul sadness

Often we find it difficult to claim happiness as our right because life hides us from that Soul truth. Life also hides us from ourselves. The older we get the more our conscious mind rules our life, and the less attention we give to the voice in our heart. Our life gets filled with haste, distraction, drama, having, doing. We become more and more responsible, with careers, mortgages, children, partners. More often than not our life gets too full for us! We become so out of balance that we end up disconnected from who we really are. We snuff out our light. We forget happiness is ours already. Really it's a Soul disconnection. Soul sadness.

Every moment spent living out-of-tune with our truth causes Soul sadness. Soul sadness often manifests as depression, anxiety and overwhelm. Times in my life when I've experienced Soul sadness were characterised by an underlying emptiness, exhaustion, floods of baseless tears, and persistently urgent feelings of needing to find an indefinable 'something'. Me.

When Soul happiness is absent, we become trapped in cycles of fleeting happiness. We do things we think we have to. We strive for other people's storybook happiness instead of our own. We fill our lives with things, because we are conditioned to think that happiness is success. We forget happiness is our right. And we end up living the shadow lives I discuss later in this book.

The circumstances that most contribute to Soul disconnection are discussed in detail in *Beyond Happiness*. They are summarised below.

Life layers

Consider for a moment that you are a bright shining being; imagine you glow brighter than the sun. See yourself as that bright light. Now consider all the negative words, people, places, events and situations you have experienced in your life so far. Consider all the things that have upset you in the past and all the things you're worried about in the future. These form what I call the 'layers of life'. These life layers wrap around you like the layers of an onion or the delicate web of a chrysalis. They create such an opaque shell that it's likely you can't even see your shining true self inside. Life has hidden from you your pure light, your true self, and your happiness within. When we live our lives within the tight bounds of the life layers that shape us, we are constricting our spirits.

Our deeply held beliefs, patterns and values, most of which are rooted in our deep subconscious and programmed from an early age, create layers around our shining true selves. Life layers hide us. And we must move through our layers in order to discover who we really are, and then what our purpose is.

Distraction

We fill our lives with distraction, and our focus and attention is mostly turned outward. We clutter our minds with constant chatter and negative thoughts, letting things like television and the Internet overstimulate us. We neglect our physical bodies, feeding them unhealthy food, layering them in chemicals, and depriving them of breath. We hide our true selves in a cloud of consuming emotions like fear, worry, and self-doubt. And we deny our spirits by ignoring the whispers of our hearts.

Such distraction is only distracting us from ourselves and from being present with our own spirits. It distracts us from seeing the beauty of ourselves. So many of us feel disconnected from our true selves. But the thing is, once we release the need for distraction in our lives, not only do we create space and time for ourselves, we find ourselves again.

Others

At an early age we learn to modify our thoughts, behaviour and even our choices to please others. This learned behaviour sticks and we grow up afraid of honouring who we are. So many of us end up living our lives based on what we think other people might think of us. Foremost, our parents shape us. Sometimes we are so desperate for their approval and love that we live our lives the way we believe they think we should. What our friends, colleagues, and even the media think is best for us also influences us. Sometimes we are so busy pleasing other people that we give away ownership of our lives. We ignore our inner voices and let others' opinions divert us from our paths.

What I've learnt for myself is that the moment I stopped living my life according to what other people thought and instead started being true to who I really was, I finally felt free. Being true to who you really are is the ultimate freedom. Now is the time to give up living your life according to other people's expectations.

Self-belief

We hear of the words 'lack mentality' used in relation to money, usually referring to a reason why people feel like they don't have enough. But we also have a lack mentality about ourselves. We think we're not that special. Or gifted. Or talented. Or unique. We think we're not blessed. We often fail to recognise our distinctive talents, our special strengths, our innate gifts because we lack self-worth and self-love and because we suppress our own light. We often take things about ourselves for granted. We assume that everyone is like us, that we're not so distinctively special at all. We say no to ourselves, talk ourselves down, and keep ourselves playing small every day.

Well I've got news for you! You are gifted, talented and blessed beyond belief. That's why you're here. To see the beauty and brilliance of your true self. And to shine in the world. These virtues link intrinsically with your Soul purpose. Recognising them connects you more strongly to your true self. This world needs that special something that only you can give. Be grateful for yourself and all your amazing gifts.

Crave meaning

It is likely you – like so many others throughout time – have pondered the meaning of life. If not, now is the time to starting craving a deeper awareness and meaning of your life. This deep desire for understanding will guide you where you need to go.

Who are we? Where do we come from? Why are we here? What is the point of life? Who is looking out for me? Am I in control of my own life or is my destiny pre-determined?

These questions are really designed to help us connect to our deepest happiness, and yet it seems we ask them even more deeply and fervently when things go wrong. We feel forsaken, and question why a higher power would let bad things happen.

So, who are we? In recent times, the prevailing view has been that the human being is little more than a complex biological and physiological mechanism. In other words, science believes us to be nothing more than sophisticated machines with an inbuilt programme to streamline survival and reproduction. Our ability to have spiritual experiences, or to be deeply moved by the simple beauty of a single flower, are seen as mere spin-offs of our highly developed, functioning brains. Science would have us believe there is no Soul.

But I for one find it hard to match my own experiences and beliefs to the scientific model. I believe the Soul is eternal and exists outside of space and time. And it is not just me. Philosophers throughout time have talked of the eternal nature of the Soul as something that defies simple biology, that transcends death and that has its home on a higher plane.

You crave meaning because you are a spiritual being and you can't have lifelong happiness while also denying your spirit and stifling your inner voice.

Believe you have purpose. Accept that your presence in this time and place is not an accident. And know that happiness is yours. They are all beautifully intertwined.

The music of your Soul

Everyone has a plan for Soul happiness. It's like an encoded Soul blueprint for your life containing the deepest secrets about who you are. I call it your

Soul code, and the following chapters will help you decipher yours.

Here's another way to think of it. It's like you are the musician, the instrument and the music in one. The musician is your true self. The instrument represents your unique gifts and virtues. The music is your path and purpose.

The musician learns, practices and applies their knowledge, always focused on their goal. The instrument is always fit-for-purpose; it is designed to produce a specific sound. The music exists but can only be shared when the musician and instrument become one.

The only difference between a high school band saxophonist and the star performer in a symphony orchestra is the connection, dedication and focus of the musician. The musician makes the music sing when they become one with the instrument. Their power to move others is magnified when they join with other musicians. It's a beautiful thing. And so is the music of your Soul.

And yet, you can easily be out-of-tune and off-key. In fact, too many of us are. And you will know. The music produced by such an instrument usually sounds and feels awful. Discordant and uncomfortable. That's because when you are off-path, unaware of your own brilliance, and disconnected from who you really are, life is a bumpy road instead of a smooth flow.

You can still live a serviceable life out of tune. Most people do. You can still function. You can still have enjoyment and happiness. You can still love. But most of it will be fleeting. And mostly you will be left with a deep emptiness and an unexplainable, underlying feeling of searching for more. The thing you are searching for is your true self and your true purpose, and these are the elements of Soul happiness.

The moment you bring yourself back into alignment with who you really are and what your purpose really is, well that's the moment you fill every part of your life with the sweetness and beauty of your spirit. That's when you claim Soul happiness as your right.

Simple reflection

It is important that you take the time now to explore your thoughts, feelings and views on purpose and Soul happiness.

Ponder the following questions and spend time recording your thoughts in the Soul Happiness companion workbook or your journal.

- Do you believe you have a right to happiness in your life? Why?
- What does Soul happiness mean to you? How do you describe or define it for yourself?
- Have you ever experienced moments of Soul disconnection or Soul sadness in your life? Describe some of those moments and how you felt.
- How have the circumstances described on pages 6-8 limited you?
- What other circumstances are keeping you from being claiming happiness as your right?

Simple promise

Make this simple promise to yourself now. Remind yourself of this promise throughout your day or write it down where you will see it.

I am worthy of blissful, life-long happiness.

Simple practices

To create the space for Soul happiness, you need to create time, space and balance in your life. *Beyond Happiness* was written to help you do just that. But if you haven't had the chance to read it yet, here are some simple tips to start.

Calm your mind. Harness the creative power of your mind. Use positive words and thoughts, and be grateful in life and for life.

Balance your body. Bring your physical body into a state of energised balance. See yourself with loving eyes, balance your energy systems, hydrate yourself well, breathe, and nourish yourself inside and out with healthy, organic foods and products.

Free your emotions. Free yourself from the emotions of hurt, fear and disappointment and infuse your life with love and beauty. Release your hurts with love, surround yourself with people who uplift you, and deeply love and accept every part of yourself.

Connect with your spirit. Take the time to see the truth of who you are. Give yourself permission to create time in your life for you. And then actually do it. Make a regular 'you' date. Treasure yourself, pamper yourself, take a walk, sit under a tree, read an inspiring book, meditate, create. Do whatever your spirit calls you to do with this special you time.

simple meditation

Welcome Happiness

Get comfortable in your meditation space.

Breathe in through your nose and out through your mouth.

Breathe deeply and feel all tension leave you.

Breathe deeply. Draw in peace.

Bathe in blissful energy. Relax.

Release all heaviness from your heart.

Let worry, fear and regret float gently away.

Love heals you. Purifies you. All is well.

Life's delicate wonder and beauty infuses you.

Give thanks. Allow gifts to bless you, always.

Open your heart to you. All of you.

Feel the radiance of your true essence.

Let divine love nourish your spirit.

You are love. You are joy. You are happiness.

Abundantly. Eternally. Beautifully.

And so it is.

CHAPTER 2

secret 2: the soul's natural order

Only the dreamer knows the dream.
~ Carl Jung

Just as there is a natural order and cycle to everything in nature, so is there a natural symmetry and structure to our Soul nature.

Think about the way the sun rises and sets, the way a woman's body knows exactly what to do to nurture the baby growing within, the way so many animals instinctively return to their own place of birth to reproduce or to die, the way plants know when to flower based on the season. There are no programmes for this. No one telling the sun what to do, or taking the animals and showing them the way home, or flicking a switch on an apple tree so it starts fruiting. Imagine the disharmony and disorder there would be on this beautiful planet of ours if these cycles had no structure or order. These things happen, naturally, effortlessly, because they are innate. They just *are*.

And your Soul just *is* too. It has its own natural order in place to help you flow with ease through life.

Order is created by your Soul code, which is the unique suite of Soul assets you bring into each incarnation, and your Soul purpose, which is your reason for being in this lifetime. The closer your path is to your natural Soul order, the more life flows.

I am reminded of this nearly constantly in my own life. When I am focused on my purpose, and I'm clear about my path – the steps I'm taking to express my purpose – life hums along. I make more money, I have more inspiration, I am more productive, I feel more connected, and loving, and inexplicably happy to my core.

I call it Soul flow. It's when you are resonating, living, so in tune with who you really are that the Universe brings you everything you need.

But there have been plenty of times where I have been stagnating, and even blocking that Soul flow. In the early days because I wasn't consciously aware of my purpose, and sometimes because my decisions take me out of flow and off path.

It reminds me of a road trip my husband Mac and I did in England. With the warren of back roads and small villages in the area, we were extremely grateful that our car had a satellite navigation device installed to tell us where to go. It was the kind that directs you with a visual map and verbal instructions, which were spoken aloud in a woman's voice. We affectionately called her 'Barbara'.

Barbara was always trying to get us where we needed to go in the most efficient, expedient way. If we took a wrong turn or missed an exit, she would helpfully recalculate a new route for us. Sometimes we went miles and miles off course, but we always got back on the path and always reached our destination in the end.

If I stop to think about it, my life has kind of been like that. And yours will be too. Our Soul is the navigation device itself, with a natural order and unique coding and purpose. We have free will to choose our own path, and yet if we veer too far off course our very own 'Barbara' – our intuition or inner guide – lets us know and tries to get us back on path.

I've learnt that life itself is about learning, understanding and moving forward. Though the whole path may not be clear, with each step you take forward it becomes a little more illuminated. In exactly the same way as Barbara only ever focused on one part of our journey at a time.

Most of us have no idea how beautifully powerful we really are when we stand in the light of our true selves. In reality our Soul purpose is so great that we rarely glimpse the final destination because the more we grow, the more it grows. Rather, your Soul almost drip feeds your purpose to you. It's like every step, the volume gets turned up a notch so you can see and hear and feel even more clearly.

The Soul's code

We are here to gain wisdom and reach our highest potential. In life, we seek to go higher, do better, be more. The natural urge to grow is an inherent part of our Soul-self. Your Soul is pure light and love. And the more connected you are to this part of you, the lighter and brighter you become. The more on purpose and on path you are, the more you literally become full of light. Enlightened.

This is why so many of us feel inexplicably drawn to a higher path or calling. The desire to live our greatest life is a deep part of who we are. It is so intrinsic that the absence of knowing our path causes more than our fair share of challenges, difficulty, separation, even heartache. That's because you are an eternal Soul gathering lessons and learning to help you grow.

Why then does it feel so hard? Why doesn't everyone know what they're here to learn and give, and just do it?

The answer is simple: because looking deeper, trusting your inner guidance, finding your own answers, mastering your lessons, and having the courage to live your truth are part of the purpose itself.

But we have been given the blueprints. Every Soul has a unique code. The Soul code. Just as the physical you has a unique make-up according to your cellular DNA; your Soul has a unique make-up according to your spiritual DNA.

Your Soul code offers the blueprint for discovering your Soul purpose – or, rather, allowing it to find you – as well as the tools for expressing it and reaching your fullest potential in this lifetime. The Soul code can differ from lifetime to lifetime.

Your Soul code is the unique suite of Soul assets you bring into each incarnation. Think of it as the bag, or toolkit you've packed full of everything you need for this 'sleepover'.

Your Soul code is the expression of who you are in this lifetime. It is the essence of who you are at the purest level.

There are four aspects to the Soul code and the chapters that follow will guide you to unlock each area of your own Soul code.

Soul challenges: what you are here to learn, the lessons you are mastering to help with Soul growth. Often linked to inner purpose.

Soul values: our inherent values and beliefs, closely linked to our feelings about ourselves and others, and influential in the choices we make.

Soul character: sometimes also referred to as spirit – our unique traits, gifts, qualities, personality, spark and zest. Our character is usually innate.

Soul path: Soul path is the trail of breadcrumbs in our life, helping us to connect to our Soul truth and Soul purpose.

Destiny or decision

About now you are probably thinking, *Am I in charge of my life? How much is chance, how much is luck, how much is choice and how much is destiny?* Let me answer these questions simply for you.

There is no great mystery. You are in charge. Completely. You have free will and you can make any decision you want. You also have the ability to create the life you want and live the life of your dreams.

The key is to ensure the life you want aligns with your highest truth, your Soul purpose. Because when your choices are based on the mind's illusions about what it means to be successful, or loved, or happy, that is not really your truth. You get out of alignment with your true self and your true purpose. That's when – to the outside world – you seem to have the most perfect life, yet you feel empty, lost and anxious inside.

So what are we here for? Simple. We are here for love. That is our *sole* purpose and our *Soul* purpose. If we could master that, we would be fast-tracked through earth's Soul school.

Let's break down the Soul's earth journey in simple terms.

Earth's Soul school provides unlimited opportunities for awakening and enlightenment. Just like every successive year in school, the higher you go at Soul school, the more you draw on your accumulated knowledge, and the greater the lessons. Lessons that are mastered over lifetimes then become the gifts that you use in service to others.

The context – or to use an education term, the 'curriculum' – that the learning follows is *purpose*. And your purpose is based more on who you choose to be, rather than what you do.

There is a difference between your Soul purpose and your life path.

Your Soul purpose is different for every lifetime. But it always has the same essence – love. Trust that when it comes to your Soul plan for this stint in earth school, you have already agreed the most important details and you've made sure you have everything you need.

Yet with every incarnation you also have free will to set your own life path. You choose in every moment how you will express yourself and how you will live your life.

As I described in *Beyond Happiness*, you are not just a bystander with a predetermined purpose; you also have the ability to create the life of your dreams.

If your life were like a book, then the entire library would be our unified

> *Soul purpose of love. Your life story [path] would be the book, and your Soul purpose is like the overall theme of the book. Within the book, there are numerous chapters and sections, each representing a different aspect of your life. You can write every one of those chapters.*

The mistake that most of us make is failing to connect our life path (the choices we make for ourselves) with our Soul purpose (our highest intention for this lifetime). It's like failing to realise the overall theme of the book before you start writing. The longer this discord continues, the more life becomes mismatched and confusing, and it's inevitable that we become out of sync with who we really are.

There are multiple paths to the same destination. You choose how you get there. Like any journey, there's the long way around and the short way. There's the bumpy road and the smooth road. There's the road with detours and the road with multiple pit stops. The choice is always yours.

But when you are on the path of your Soul purpose, life flows, wishes are answered, dreams become reality and everything seems magical. And why? Because you are living in tune with your Soul plans for this lifetime.

The multiplicity of purpose

Instead of just one purpose in life, we actually have four. I use 'Soul purpose' to refer to them all collectively. And each of those four aspects of purpose has multiple levels of complexity depending on the level of progress we make in this life.

The four aspects of our purpose are **inner purpose, outer purpose, shared purpose** and **divine purpose**. We fulfil our Soul purpose when we unlock every area.

Within each of those four aspects, there are multiple levels of growth depending on how much you apply the Principles of Soul Growth (see chapter 11). The faster we progress on our path, the more we open ourselves to an even deeper realisation of who we really are and what we are really here to do.

We are beings of mind, body, emotion *and* spirit and only have complete wellbeing when every level of our whole self is in harmony.

Similarly, we need balance across all four aspects of our purpose for higher wellbeing. Every aspect of our purpose is so intertwined it is nearly impossible to talk about one without the other, or fulfil one without the other.

We cannot fulfil our outer purpose without first awakening to who we truly are. We cannot awaken to who we truly are without harnessing our higher guidance. And we need all three to make our shared contribution to humanity.

Purpose is as beautifully complex and connected as the levels of our being. There are direct connections between the four aspects of purpose and the four aspects of our being and Soul happiness unfurls when we bring every aspect of ourselves and our purpose into harmony.

Let's go deeper into each aspect of purpose.

Inner purpose

Inner purpose is about discovering you. It is the inner journey to the truest, purest you; your Soul-self. It is the most important aspect of our purpose, and the only aspect that will bring lasting happiness.

Our inner purpose is about honouring ourselves, awakening to who we truly are and connecting to our spirit. It is connected to the 'emotional' aspect of our being because the challenge is to unconditionally love ourselves. It's about being authentically you so you can get down to the business of doing what you are here to do.

Inner purpose is closely linked to our life lessons and, therefore, the path within can be full of challenges. Most significantly the challenge of seeing what is really true in our lives. Inner purpose is about moving through the life layers I describe in *Beyond Happiness*. Life layers are the deeply held belief systems that surround, even encase us. It's like layers of an onion wrapped about beautiful shining you at the core.

The path of inner purpose can be long, as the more we resist the harder it becomes to go within. Some people never move past inner purpose. They get stuck, or blocked, and unable to start living their true outer purpose.

Everything is intertwined and cyclical. Realising your inner purpose doesn't mean those lessons stop. It means you approach life with a deeper awareness of who you are, and a greater acceptance of what is. In my own case I found that my lessons seem to repeat, calling me to go deeper still. It's as though the Universe just wants to check that I've 'got it'. The further I go with my outer purpose, the more I am confronted by my own inner journey. There are some beliefs and patterns about myself and my life – usually of the self-limiting kind – that run pretty deep within.

However, just as our outer purpose expands outwardly the more we grow and evolve, I also believe that our inner purpose fine-tunes inwardly, ensuring we experience an ever brighter spotlight on the truth of who we really are, on every level of our being.

For example, I found that if I became aware of a lesson on the physical level and released and let go of the need for it there, eventually the same lesson would present itself on the mental level, then the emotional level, then the spiritual level, before it could finally be released and passed on altogether.

So the path of inner purpose is this: awareness of patterns of behaviour, thought, emotion that are blocking Soul flow... Which leads to insight of the lesson(s) underlying the pattern... Which requires a commitment to embody learning on a mental, physical, emotional and spiritual level... Which leads to a deeper connection to your Soul-self.

Inner purpose is even greater than outer purpose, because it is only through living life as we truly are, free of the facades created by perception, judgement and expectation, that we can step into our full Soul power. It is this inner presence – our inner awakening and knowing – coupled with the energy and vitality it creates, that gives us everything we need to fulfil our outer purpose.

You know you are being called to honour your inner purpose when:

- You feel disconnected from who you are
- You are significantly overweight
- You feel an unexplained weight on your shoulders
- You feel suffocated
- You know you should feel happier
- You frequently cry for no reason
- You often feel sad, low, even depressed and you don't know why
- You are quick to anger and you feel like you can't control it
- You have the same reoccurring patterns or problems in your life
- Life feels harder than it should be.

Outer purpose

Where inner purpose is about being in service to yourself, outer purpose is about being in service to others. Outer purpose is the highest expression of your own unique talents, qualities, gifts, passions and values.

Outer purpose is connected to the 'mind' because it is often the ego – its illusions, its trappings, the cycles of fleeting happiness in which it ensnares us – that shape our journey towards realising this aspect of ourselves.

Outer purpose is like your own personal Soul mission. Some of us fully step into that Soul mission, some of us just get across the line, and some of us never get there at all. Too bogged down with self-limiting belief, inner purpose issues and an extra thick wadding of life layers.

Outer purpose can be expressed on a multitude of levels. The call to be in service to others may start at an immediate level close to home. In time it may progress to a community. Then you reach may touch a country, then a continent. And eventually you may find yourself working for collective humanity. The only limitations are your own.

Knowing, discovering, finding your outer purpose is rarely a big reveal. Often we are already living the shadow of our true purpose.

Often we see one part of the path at the time. One stepping stone at a time. When we achieve what we intended to on each part of the path, it triggers the illumination of the next stepping stone. Why? Because our potential is greater than we can imagine. So we are gently guided, step-by-step. And as part of the path we set ourselves a myriad of tests. All the things we want to make doubly, triply and sometimes (in my case at least) endlessly sure we have learnt before our Soul-self allows us to take the next step of outer purpose.

The key with outer purpose is to understand that it is not about doing the things you think you must to make you happy. As Jesus put it, "gain the world and lose your Soul."

You have to know how to be happy without the success, recognition or rewards you will gain from fulfilling your outer purpose. The things we feel we have to do to make us happy come from our ego self. The solution is, do whatever you do in the world for joy and because it resonates with your Soul truth, not because of the rewards it may bring.

You know it is time to honour your outer purpose when:

- You feel called to work in service of others
- You feel alive, excited, tingly when you think of your dreams and passions
- You feel completely disconnected from your current work, career or life situation
- You have everything you want but feel little true joy or happiness in your life
- You feel resentful about how you 'have' to spend your time
- You feel like there's something you're 'supposed' to be doing but you don't know what

- You are fearful of change or new opportunities
- You find yourself zoning out during meetings or conversations
- You experience regular conflict with others
- You feel like people just don't 'get you'.

Shared purpose

Shared purpose is the same for all humanity; a unified purpose to embody love and spread joy. In doing so we create world happiness. Love is like the currency of the Universe. It is the energy from which we all derive and it is the underlying source of all life force.

Our shared purpose is connected to the 'physical' aspect of our being, because it is anchored in the present. The more of us that consciously tap into our higher guidance and live Soul-centred lives, the more we lift the vibration of the whole planet.

When you align your inner and outer self, you fall into the natural rhythm of shared purpose. You do not have to do anything more. By living your true purpose in tune with who you really are, and embodying love and joy in everything that you do, you give others the permission to do the same. A favourite quote of mine is from Ghandi: "Be the change you wish to see in the world". People want to emulate what they see. So, when you are living a life of bliss, you lift others around you to do the same, and soon the whole vibe of the planet will change.

It's like a gradual blooming of all the roses in a beautiful garden. Some are not getting the attention or nourishment they need. Some are struggling to reach high enough for the sun. While others have everything they need, are bathed in sunlight every day and find themselves growing tall and strong. They blossom and share their beauty and heal the world.

Some people choose to combine their outer purpose with shared purpose. These people act like beacons of goodness and love in the world, shining light where it is needed most.

When we are all living in harmony with our unified purpose – pure, unadulterated love – there will be world peace and world happiness. Be you. Be love. Be joy. Change the world. You have the power. Just like the magnificent ant, a tiny creature with superpower-like capabilities to move mountainous obstacles in its path, one person can truly make a difference.

World happiness starts with you. Inner peace creates outer peace. Outer peace creates world peace. Simple.

You know you are honouring your shared purpose when:

- You feel a love for humanity
- You feel inexplicably drawn to help others on a world stage
- Others are easily drawn to you
- You feel a deep connection to those in need
- You feel joy in every moment.

Divine purpose

Your divine purpose in this life is to evolve into the full sixth sensory version of you. Sixth sensory living, or Soulful living as I call it, is a deeply essential part of stepping into your full power.

It is connected to the 'spirit' aspect of your being, because in unlocking your divine purpose you create a direct hotline to your higher self.

I believe we are all sixth sensory beings. Those gifts are not just bestowed on a select few. We all have them. Even the most doubtful or ego-bound among us still make decisions based on gut instinct or intuition (although the true source of their wisdom is rarely acknowledged). The truth is, every single one of us is blessed with the Soul gifts of sacred perception, insight and connection to a higher source. Most of us are on the cusp of awakening to who we truly are.

This divine purpose is really the key to discovering and then living your purpose. It is our sixth sense that propels us rapidly along our path and guides us higher still. It is like our secret inner power – or if we were super heroes, our super power – that makes the impossible possible. It's like adding rocket fuel to your life. You are going to get where you're going a heck of a lot easier and faster.

While I will weave using your intuition throughout this book, unlocking your sixth sensory gifts is such a vast topic that it is the subject of the third book in this series.

You know your divine purpose is ready to be embraced if:

- You have frequent and exceptionally vivid dreams
- You feel the same thoughts over and over again but ignore them
- You think of someone only to have them text, call or email
- You think of something and it happens
- You feel an unexplained sense of urgency
- You feel exceptionally sensitive to other people's moods and emotions
- You feel overwhelmed in public places or crowded social situations
- You experience frequent synchronicity
- People just show up with what it is you're looking for
- You have had an angelic or spiritual experience.

Soul path and purpose

There's been a lot of information in this chapter, so let's sum it up.

- Prior to coming into this life, you set a Soul purpose and established the Soul code that will support it.
- Ultimately these plans are about what you need to learn, how you will serve, and what you choose to experience.
- Your purpose comprises four aspects – inner purpose, outer purpose, shared purpose and divine purpose.
- Freewill is one of the spiritual laws that ensures the learning and development of the Soul, and you use it to set your life path.

- Freewill allows you to constantly make choices and decisions about every part of your life.
- You inner guidance is the compass helping you to honour yourself and stay connected to your purpose.
- The more your life choices are in alignment with your Soul code and purpose, the more you are in Soul flow and Soul happiness is inevitable.
- The less your choices are in alignment, the more confusion and disconnection you feel and the harder things become.

What you most need to realise is that your whole life, every moment, is about purpose. Soul purpose and, therefore, Soul happiness, goes so much deeper. Fulfilling our inner purpose is the most important, and yet the hardest thing to do. We get so preoccupied with the outer aspect of our life, and what we are here to do, that we forget first to *be*. The being is our greatest challenge, and it is why we must realise our inner purpose before we can live our outer purpose.

Inner purpose is about power. Outer purpose is about passion. Only through your inner purpose do you discover the strength, energy, vitality and true essence of yourself to bring your outer purpose into being. Your outer purpose is the perfect combination of everything you are – your gifts, talents, qualities and values. The fusion of this inner power and outer passion reveal your purpose. You don't create your purpose. You don't discover your purpose. It already is. It presents itself when you are ready. It reveals itself. You choose to live it.

So you see, you can be neither on the path or off the path. You are the path. The path is you. Awakening to yourself is the purpose.

✻

Simple reflection

This reflection time is designed to help you gauge your current experience of Soul purpose in your life.

- In your journal, draw a simple graph. On one axis number 1-10. On the other axis add four headings: inner, outer, shared and divine. You can also use the Soul Happiness companion workbook for this exercise.
- Consider the statements on pages 21-27.
- Allocate one point for every statement in the inner purpose, outer purpose and divine purpose lists that feels true for you right now. Allocate two points for every true statement in the shared purpose list to get a value out of 10.
- Plot your results on your graph.
- The results will tell you several things. The flatter your graph is, the more in balance you are across every aspect of your purpose. Higher scores indicate you are being drawn to look at this part of your purpose right now.
- What does this graph reveal to you? What have you learnt about yourself through this exercise?

Simple promise

Make this simple promise to yourself now. Remind yourself of this promise throughout your day or write it down where you will see it.

I open my heart to receive my highest guidance for my purpose in this life.

Simple practice

These simple steps can help you put the ideas in this chapter into practice. Remember, there is power in doing something. Anything. Just one thing. Because the moment you do, you make a conscious change in your life.

Decree. Decide that you are ready to know your Soul purpose. By doing so you invite the Universe to bring you the answer and start showing you the steps.

Tune in. Take steps to actively start tuning into your higher guidance. Practice breathing, meditation, journaling or any other activities that see you enjoy silence and stillness in which to receive insights.

Act. Even now you are likely resisting something in your life and you will be receiving repetitive thoughts and feelings around it. Take the step and others will be revealed.

Balance. Decide how you can bring balance to every part of your purpose – inner, outer, shared and divine. Perhaps you may plan a regular 'date' with yourself to explore your inner journey. Or start unexpected random acts of kindness to selflessly serve others. Or pick up litter in your street or your local park. Or start reading a sixth sensory book. There are many small steps you can take towards balancing and revealing your purpose.

CHAPTER 3

secret 3: lessons have purpose

The wound is the place where the Light enters you.
~ Rumi

The aspect of your Soul code we will explore in this chapter is Soul challenges. Soul challenges are the things we are here to learn to help with Soul growth. It's about mastering life's lessons.

Inner awareness of these challenges allows you to become your own greatest teacher and master of your destiny. I truly believe that.

I feel I have a lot of lessons in this lifetime, and perhaps you do too. The most significant lesson I'm aware of for myself is unconditional self-love. I'm still working on it and I feel like perhaps I always will be. Just when I think I've got it, another aspect presents itself. I wrote about aspects of my self-love in *Beyond Happiness*. But I get the sense this is a major lesson for me as aspects of it seem to be permanently on repeat.

Even as a child I was solitary. I remember feeling as though I didn't quite fit in and looking at the other kids wondering what they didn't like about me and why they didn't seem to want to be my friend. I have always felt a desperate need for people to like me. My self-protection mechanisms kicked in at an early age and to avoid judgement, rejection and even teasing I learnt to keep myself to myself. I had friends. But I just didn't put myself out there. I was reserved. Contained. I held myself tightly.

My most upsetting life memories seem to involve friendships or relationships with others. Between the ages of 13 and 18, I was unceremoniously dumped by three successive groups of school friends. Usually the conversations were along the lines of *We don't like you, you're not cool enough, we don't want you to hang out with us anymore.*

To a teenager that kind of rejection is not only baffling, it's Soul destroying. It's hard to work out what you did wrong or what those 'friends' didn't like about you. And it's hard to pick yourself up the next day (and the day after that, and the day after that) and keep on living. It might sound a little melodramatic, but it wasn't. I battled for years with destructive doubts and damaging thoughts. *Well if no one likes you, what is the point of being here at all?*

I had a resilience of spirit even then, and fortunately there have always been people in my life who could see the beauty of the real me, long before I ever could.

As I've progressed into adulthood the same friendship patterns followed me. And the pattern extended past friendships into relationships. At times, if I'm honest, it feels like I have been surrounded by people that held little value of me, didn't respect or honour me, took advantage of my desire to be 'liked', and really didn't love me at all. As much as I wanted them to.

Sometimes I look with longing at those people who have had the same tight-knit circle of friends since childhood. Or those people that fell in love and married their high school sweetheart and lived happily ever after. But I also firmly believe there is a reason or a purpose in everything. And there's something about me and friendships that has been stuck a bit too permanently on repeat for this to not be a Soul lesson.

It hasn't been until the last few years that I've finally been able to see what the lesson or, in this case, lessons are. And for me, that lesson is unconditional self-love. I'm still learning. The insights that I've had as part of this learning have been that the friendships and relationships in my life have precisely mirrored my own inner feelings about myself. If I believed I wasn't worth respecting or valuing, I attracted people who took advantage of my goodness. If I believed I wasn't lovable, I attracted people who cheated on me or hurt me. If I believed there was nothing to value or like about myself, I seemed to attract people who brought out the worst in me.

I've learnt that in order to unconditionally love myself, I actually need to be my own best friend. I needed to love, value, honour, respect, trust and believe in myself first. I also saw how this lack of self-love manifested into habits and behaviours in my life. Like, continually moulding myself, my thoughts, actions, activities, even my style of dress, on other people to try and be liked.

When you realise you have a choice and that patterns like this aren't just your 'lot' in life, things start to shift. A major moment of self-love for me was leaving my first marriage because I knew it wasn't right. When you honour yourself by taking a Soul-driven action such as this, you change the vibration you are sending out. And that new vibration was perfect for attracting my gorgeous Soul love, Mac. The more I honour and love myself and have the courage to let go of the need to be liked and to just be me, the more I have attracted the truest friends I've ever had.

There are always gifts hidden in our challenges too. I've realised I have a strength of spirit and a resilience that defies all odds. I've realised that my higher senses are finely tuned and always have been. I've replaced my false beliefs with a Soul truth. I've realised I'm pretty amazing, and because of that, I am surrounded by amazing people too.

When we think of life purpose or our reason for being here on this planet right now, most people think it's about what we are here to *do*. And yes, it's important to consider how we will make a difference for others, and what sort of legacy we'll leave behind (which are both related to our outer purpose).

But more important is *who* we are here to be. To know that, we need to know ourselves. And to know ourselves we need to understand our lessons and unbundle our false beliefs.

Soul cycles of learning

Inner awareness, or self-awareness, is about understanding who you truly are. Inner awareness and inner purpose are closely infused. They are about awakening to you.

To awaken we have to learn. And so we have set ourselves Soul challenges. We have a myriad of lessons to learn across every part of our life. They are as individual as we are.

Everything is connected. Lessons provide us with awareness, and awareness unlocks our inner knowing and the gifts you need to step into your purpose.

There is a duality of purpose that is to learn and to be of service. And often, as I have discovered for myself, we need to learn *before* we can be of service. Mastering our lessons is important because it enables us to use our gifts and talents for the good of others. To become the teacher. So to be of service to others through our outer purpose we must first see and then master the inner lessons we have chosen for ourselves in this lifetime.

There is a spiritual structure to our learning. A logic to our lesson plan. You have been in Soul school, learning from the Soul curriculum, throughout many lifetimes, and with each incarnation you progress. You can choose to move through your lessons as quickly or as slowly as you wish according to your freewill.

To embody our lessons every Soul must past through four stages:

Novice

If you are a novice, situations and experiences will be completely new and feel quite challenging to your current way of thinking or living. To determine whether or not you are a novice, look at how much challenge, frustration or suffering you have. The more you have, the higher the likelihood you are a novice at this lesson. You can't see the lesson.

Apprentice

If you are an apprentice, you will feel like you've been here before. Perhaps there are cycles and patterns that keep repeating over, and over again, or stresses and challenges that seem to be the constant theme in your life. As an apprentice you can see the lesson, just not the way to master it. You are open to learning it, and may even seek help to do so but there will be an underlying level of resistance to change. You can see the lesson but don't act, you resist the learning. You know you are at the end of your apprenticeship when you feel the shift inside you to do something differently.

Master

If you are a master, you are fully open to the learning and most likely connected to your inner guidance on the lesson. It means that you embrace what you are learning, and actively seek to grow from it. You see that the lessons are really a projection of yourself, and in order to learn you must grow within. To be a master we need to look beyond our perception of the reason for the lesson, and see the real truth of why. And then choose to do something differently.

Teacher

If you are a teacher, you have so fully mastered the particular lesson that it ceases to affect your life in any way. It is simply remembering what you already know. You generally feel so much clarity that you feel detached from the lesson, whereas novices, apprentices, and masters may feel varying degrees of being absorbed by it. You can see the big picture, whereas they may be unable to 'see the wood for the trees'. Teachers are able to share the wisdom of their knowledge and inspire others. Often it is the lessons that you have already explored in previous lifetimes – as a novice, then apprentice and then master – that you become a teacher of in this lifetime. Those qualities or traits become your gifts and often feed into your outer purpose.

So there is a clear path through every challenging situation and every lesson. And that path is about acceptance, learning and detachment. The more you embrace your lessons, and see their ultimate connection to your Soul purpose, the more freedom you will gain.

The 12 Soul lessons

When you shift your perspective from seeing things that happen to you as annoyingly repetitive, or simply bad luck, to seeing them as lessons, that moment of awareness allows you to become more attentive to your lessons and make choices that can accelerate your learning. You also discover that in your lessons usually lie your gifts.

The thing is, you are required to set your own course through this school of sacred learning and work autonomously, at your own pace, in your own time. You have an unlimited source of loving guidance on hand to help you out.

The sooner you understand what you are here to learn, the sooner you can get busy acing the class. It is usually not difficult to discern your life lessons. It takes a sense of self-awareness and some inner reflection. And that is it. The more challenging aspect is doing something with what you discover.

There are 12 common Soul lessons, each presenting themselves in endless variations throughout our lives. I share them here to start your own inner reflection process. May they lead you to even deeper insights.

- **Detachment.** Separating from the need for things, approval, recognition and success in order to feel worthiness and joy.

- **Judgement.** Accepting everything as it is and everyone as they are. Everyone is divine in the eyes of God.

- **Poverty.** Releasing the mentality of lack – emotionally, spiritually, financially and more – and being open to receive abundance.

- **Thought.** Realising you create your reality by mastering your thoughts in order to create the life you want for yourself.

- **Truth.** Seeing past illusion in any part of your life to reveal your deepest truth. This also includes seeing the truth of others.

- **Faith.** Releasing fear knowing that everything is unfolding in the perfect way and at the perfect time.

- **Forgiveness.** Freeing yourself from hurt by forgiving yourself and forgiving others.

- **Trust.** Knowing you have all the answers you seek, trusting your intuition and higher guidance.

- **Belief.** Seeing your own greatness and believing you are worthy of greatness.

- **Honour.** Being self-full and living a life that authentically honours the truth of who you are.

- **Power.** Replacing the love of power with the power of love. Releasing control to empower your highest potential.

- **Love.** Deeply, unconditionally loving yourself as you do others.

As you read this list you may automatically connect with some more than others. Like for me, loving myself and others unconditionally is such a theme that it is clearly a primary lesson. Some may not resonate at all; perhaps you have already mastered that lesson.

Every step on your path of purpose will see you trigger another specific purpose-related lesson. The higher you go, sometimes the harder the lessons become. To find your flow, your path of least resistance, you need to be as closely aligned to your true self as possible.

Recognise course corrections

Nothing ever goes away until it teaches you what you need to know.
~ Pema Chodron

To be on path we must be in balance. Balance in life will also bring us a balance in purpose.

When we are out of balance in life, we will also be off path and off purpose. It is at times such as this that course correcting moments come along. Opportunities for redirection. They take many forms – illness, near death experiences, significant life changes like losing a job, and even significant people that impact our life. Redirections like this come along when we are veering significantly off path. They are designed to be big enough that they create the time, space and opportunity to get ourselves back on track.

Usually, the bigger the opportunity for course correction, the further off track we have strayed. As an example, a significant illness like cancer may be an opportunity to reconnect to your inner purpose, release patterns and belief systems that you have outgrown, and decide what you will accept as true for yourself. A near death experience may be the opportunity to reassess your values, your life, and what you are doing to make a difference for yourself and others. A significant life event, let's say losing a job, may provide the opportunity to detach from a role you have identified with and connect more deeply to who you are, what you want for yourself and what will bring you greater fulfilment. And specific people may come along to say the words and bring the guidance that your Soul team needs you to hear.

We do meet people who change our lives, who are our catalysts for Soul growth. They cross our path at the perfect moment for us to receive their lesson. Through their actions or experiences – perhaps even just the simple words they speak – we make a decision to be different. They are our earth angels, guiding us and keeping us on course.

Perhaps you've had course correcting moments? Sometimes they are crystal clear. Sometimes it doesn't become clear until years later. I've had plenty of course correcting moments. Perhaps the most significant was losing everything but my life in a house fire in my late 20s. But there have been others. And it was several years before I was to see the significance of that course correction, and the lessons and learning it held for me.

The fact is we have a natural inner compass that is always guiding us on our path. It is how we stay true. Yes we have free will, yes we are in charge, yes we are self-determining. But at a Soul level we will always be more happy and fulfilled when we are on path. The pull of that path is strong and no matter how far we stray, we will always be given the opportunity to redirect and get back on path. The choice is ours as to what we do with those opportunities.

Release false truths

Not only are we here to learn from the circumstances we are presented with, we are here to learn the truth of ourselves. Our inner lessons are the greatest.

In life, there are truths. Like you are female, or you are male. Or the sun shines during the day and the moon lights up the night. These are essential truths. And then there are false truths, or false beliefs. Like you are unlovable. Or nothing comes easy in life. Or happiness is about what you have.

False truths become deeply entrenched as part of our subconscious mental and emotional code. Usually they are imposed at such a young age that we have had no conscious choice about whether to make them our own or not. By the age of seven, most of us have formed a complete set of beliefs about ourselves and our world. They shape who we choose to be and the way we choose to live our life.

They become so deeply embedded that we wonder why we are waking up in our 20s, 30s, 40s and beyond, feeling empty, afraid, and completely disconnected from who we are. We've just spent years living someone else's life, and when it comes to living our own, we don't even know who we are, much less what we really want.

Stop for a moment and consider all the false beliefs you have hardwired into your head. To help you, let me share one of my own hardwired beliefs, which, as I've discovered, was quite opposite to my truth.

False belief: *I like meat.*
Truth: *No, I actually don't.*

The first time I even contemplated not eating meat I was in my early 30s and preparing to attend a wellbeing retreat in Australia. The retreat had strict nutrition rules, including serving vegetarian meals. For a week or two beforehand I started combining vegetarian meals into my diet because I was worried at the thought of a diet without meat. I mean seriously, *Who doesn't eat meat!?*

Well, it turned out I loved being meat-free so much that I eventually released all animal products from my diet and lifestyle – meat, dairy, eggs and more. And in all of this, do you know what I realised? I don't actually like meat. Yes. You read correctly. I do not like the taste, texture, smell or anything else about meat. And, when I stopped to examine this belief, I realised I never had.

I was confused at that. I was one of those people who would often proclaim 'I could never stop eating meat'. So where had this belief around the consumption of meat come from?

Well, I grew up on a dairy farm. Perhaps enough said. Meat was the central part of our diet and our plates would be full of it. What's interesting to me though was the way I used to eat my meat.

Picture a traditional roast beef meal. Here's what I would do. Cut a small piece of meat, load the rest of the fork up with bits of everything else on my plate, smother it in sauce or gravy and then eat it. I was not one of those people who saved their meat until last, or wolfed it down first because it was the choicest morsel. I disguised it with everything else on my plate. Why? Because I didn't like it. But I was raised to eat every scrap of food on your plate, or it would be served up cold for breakfast. I didn't have a choice, and it became hardwired as a false belief.

On nearly every level of our lives, the gap between perception and reality is vast. We think we have droopy shoulders and a wobbly bottom. Others admire the confident, sexy woman you are. We think our eyes are too small, our hair too thin, and our ears too big. Others seek to emulate your effortless natural beauty. It is easiest to use these examples on the physical level of our being, but the gap between perception and reality is just as vast at a mental, emotional and spiritual level.

The thing is our beliefs are magnetic. Our inner beliefs manifest as outer lessons. Beliefs attract with record speed our experiences. If you believe you are unworthy, unlovable, and life is all about the hard knocks, what do you think you will attract?

False beliefs hide us from our truth. They drown out who we are. They say no to the dreams in our heart. They mould us to be precisely who we are not. Usually they do not empower us to be who we really are.

And the only difference is who you think you are (perception born of beliefs) and who you really are (reality born of truth). In other words, what is real and what is not. What is real, and what is an illusion. What is real, and what is merely a fabrication of our beliefs, values, life experiences, societal pressures, and more. False beliefs create an alternate reality to the one we really should be living!

We are here to be the most expansive and free version of ourselves. Start looking at yourself and your life and some of the things you have always held true about yourself. And then start asking 'Why?'. And when you encounter something that seems false or doesn't resonate with your Soul, have the courage to choose something different for yourself.

Simple reflection

We've looked at life lessons and how they contribute to your soul growth, and we've explored false beliefs and how they can limit the expression of who we truly are. Now it is deeply important that you take the time to understand the role of lessons and learning in your own life, including beliefs that may be holding you back from who you really are.

Use your journal, or turn to the relevant page in the Soul Happiness companion workbook now.

Decoding your lessons

What am I here to learn? This is such an important question for your Soul purpose. To answer it, divide your page into four columns with the following headings: Experience, Reflection, Lessons, Action.

1. **Experiences.** Take some time to think about potential lessons in your life this far. Note these in the first column, starting each new experience on a new line.
    *   For example, are there repeating patterns, situations or events?
    *   Are you plagued by bad luck in a certain part of your life?
    *   Are there certain traits or emotions you know you need to learn from?

2. **Reflection.** Take some time to reflect on each experience or point you have noted. Ask yourself, why would this be happening in my life? Does it happen often? What do I need to see? Note your insights in the second column.

3. **Lessons.** Now try to summarise what you think the life lesson for each experience is. And then note what stage of learning you think you are at relative to this lesson – novice, apprentice, master or teacher. For example, if you have repeated failed relationships, perhaps the lesson is

to learn to love yourself and perhaps you feel you are at the apprentice stage. In this column you would write: *Unconditional Self-Love / Apprentice.*

4. **Action.** Finally, reflect on this newfound awareness. What have you learnt already? What different choices might you make? What is one thing you could do for each lesson to accelerate your learning? Note your intended actions in the fourth column.

The truth of your beliefs

- Write down any false beliefs as they are revealed to you. What beliefs did you learn as a child? Note things in your life that have always 'niggled'.

- Examine those beliefs. See where they have come from. Decide whether they are your truth, or false beliefs in disguise. Understand how they may have impacted the way you live your life.

- Let go of anything you no longer need. Use positive affirmations to clear those beliefs. Perhaps have a ceremony. Or burn them. Or rip up the paper. Something that is symbolic of the letting go process.

Simple promise

Make this simple promise to yourself now. Remind yourself of this promise throughout your day or write it down where you will see it.

I am open to seeing the gift in every lesson.

Simple practices

These simple steps can help you put the ideas in this chapter into practice. Remember, there is power in doing something. Anything. Just one thing. Because the moment you do, you make a conscious change in your life.

Have an open mind. Approach your lessons with perseverance and insight and you will move more smoothly through them.

Become flexible. Sometimes our beliefs hold us in place like concrete. Develop a more flexible approach to life. One way to do this is to become more flexible in your body. Take a yoga class, do some Pilates or try some stretching.

Make different choices. Sometimes we become fixated on the 'way' we do things. Try a different way. Make a different choice. By stepping outside our comfort zone we create a greater awareness of who we really are.

Modify your parenting approach. Understand how beliefs and values are shaped and choose to strongly nurture the true spirits of your children.

Perspective. So many things in life are a matter of perspective. Look at situations people or events in your life that may not be flowing as smoothly as you would like and see what it is within you that may be contributing to, or even creating, this situation.

Reflect. Commit to a continual cycle of reflection and deep questioning in your life. The more you do this in the moment, the greater awareness you will have of your life and your lessons. Journaling is an excellent reflective practice.

♡

simple meditation

Make Peace

Get comfortable in your meditation space.

Breathe in through your nose and out through your mouth.

Breathe deeply and feel all tension leave you.

Breathe and give thanks.

Fill your heart with beauty.

Celebrate all goodness that has passed.

Release with love all that cannot be undone.

Breathe and let go.

Arms open wide, say "Yes" to life.

See the boundless flow of opportunity.

Embrace it. Nurture it. Watch it bloom.

Become light. Be luminous. Shine.

All is beautiful. All is yours.

Perfectly. Divinely. Completely.

And so it is.

CHAPTER 4

secret 4: truth lives in your heart

Knowing who you really are is the only way to be completely happy.
~Deepak Chopra

This chapter focuses on helping you unlock the next aspect of your Soul code, your Soul values.

Soul values are the set of inherent values and beliefs that are deeply connected to who we are. They are our heart's desire, our deepest truth. They can influence how we feel about ourselves, the choices we make and the path we choose.

When you align to your core values, you can quite literally move mountains. Or in my case, more than 20 kilograms in excess weight. I spoke briefly of losing this weight in *Beyond Happiness*. I shared how I had spent most of my adult life completely disconnected from the skin I was in and how my relationship with food escalated after the traumatic house fire I survived.

I felt so unsafe in my life, so scared to be who I truly was, that I wrapped layers and layers of fat around myself as the only protection I could. I was hiding from me, and from life. And I most certainly wasn't allowing the values I so resolutely lived by in my outer life to also nurture my inner self.

The reason? Because I was carrying around a belief pattern that I was fat and unlovable. False beliefs like this have the power to overshadow values, as they did mine, and they make it difficult to be who we truly are.

Adults have no idea of the power of their flippant words. As I child I was told 'You look fat'. As teenager I was told, 'You've got nothing to be proud of'. Those projections of other people's own Soul disconnection onto me anchored so deeply. Sub-consciously, I believed I was fat and that's what I became. And I believed I was not special either. And so I settled for much less than I deserved, particularly in love and relationships. The two went hand-in-hand really. The more unlovable I felt, the more I needed to protect myself. The more I needed to protect myself, the more I ate.

Once I unbundled those beliefs, I naturally realigned to my deepest values – acceptance and freedom, beauty and love, giving and compassion. I was able to become accepting of myself, as I was so unreservedly of others. I was able to choose to live freely, in the way I wanted. I was able to nurture my own beautiful Soul by acting lovingly towards myself, with the same care and kindness I bestowed on others.

The weight-loss journey was about so much more than simply my physical body. It confronted me with all sorts of false beliefs to let go of and lessons to master. And with each pound I released I stepped a little closer to me and a little closer to my truth.

It was a recalibration with my true self, on so many levels. The weight I felt I needed to hold on to melted off as my body realigned to its natural weight. Sure, I made other changes – I joined a weight loss club and a gym and I changed my eating habits. But my ability to make those choices at that point in my life, as opposed to any other point in my adult life, was because I had unbundled the underlying beliefs feeding my weight and realigned to my values.

Some people yo-yo up and down with weight, losing it all only to pile it back on again. It's a constant battle they fight. I've kept that weight off for 10 years now, easily, without ever having to diet again. All because I unbundled the beliefs that fuelled it in the first place. With the beliefs gone there was no need for yo-yo-ing, because there was nothing feeding my need to protect myself. I could be true to who I was and live my values – inside and out. I just became me.

So many of us have no connection to our values. No idea what our own personal values may be. This chapter will guide you to make a deeper connection with your values as you take a step closer to unlocking your Soul code.

Be self-full

As you grow older, you will discover that you have two hands, one for helping yourself, the other for helping others.
~ Audrey Hepburn

The very act of contemplating who we really are, and what we really want – let alone acting on those feelings – can become challenging, because it causes us to feel selfish.

Really, selfishness is a feeling state projected onto us. Selfishness has such negative connotations that many of us strive to avoid the label by keeping our focus outward. We become scared of opinions and judgement. Scared of saying yes to ourselves and letting ourselves feel good. We stop honouring our needs, become disconnected from who we really are and move further away from our inner purpose.

To know who you are, you need to balance the inner and the outer scales in your life. You need to be neither selfish nor selfless, but self-full.

We are programmed to believe that life is all about everyone else. We think our purpose is solely about what we do, what job we have and what we do for others; how we help, care and uplift them. And it seems that very little of us, our needs or our connection to ourselves fits into that picture of 'our life'. We become selfless.

Sure we might get our hair done. Buy ourselves new things. Take holidays. Treat ourselves. But when life is so focused on giving to other people, we need to stop and ask ourselves, *What am I really giving to me?*

Being selfless unbalances us. Being selfish unbalances us. Being self-full is the perfect balance we seek. Life is only about everyone else after we have honoured ourselves. To some people this might seem selfish. But in reality, living a selfless life serves no one, least of all you. You must treasure yourself. Draw your intention inwards to self-belief, self-awareness, self-trust, self-worth and, most of all, self-love.

When we become self-full, we have the deepest insights about ourselves and the greatest awareness of our purpose. The deeper we go, the more we can see. This is our true purpose. To go within before we can turn our light outwards to be a beacon in the world.

Consider some of the remarkable, world-changing, yet seemingly selfless people in history. Mother Theresa. Mahatma Ghandi. Nelson Mandela. To name a few. These people seemed to shun their own needs, enduring suffering – even persecution – in order to selflessly make a difference for others.

To some it may seem their cause became bigger than themselves. But let's look deeper. I say these amazing people were so deeply connected to themselves, their values, their desires and their purpose that they retained their individualism; they were not conformist in any way. They had a gentle strength. An unwavering sense of self that allowed them to keep faith and focus. Fulfilling their inner purpose transcended their outer purpose.

Without their inner connection and values, these people may have stumbled, lost faith in their abilities and their goals, doubted themselves, and generally been a less solid, strong, focused version of themselves. But they knew this simple truth: all our strength comes from within.

So, do not be afraid of being self-full. Do no fear your own brilliance, your light within. Welcome a deeper Soul connection with yourself. When you do you have the energy to give to others, share your gifts with the world, and wholeheartedly live your purpose. The time to say yes to your Soul starts now.

Trust your true north

You have an inbuilt guide keeping you in alignment with your values and true beliefs: your feelings. When things feel good, it's usually because they resonate with a deeper part of you. Likewise, when things feel bad, it's usually because they are out of alignment with your Soul values. Our feelings are our true north, they guide us.

The heart generates the largest electromagnetic field in the body . . . [It's] electrical field is about 60 times greater in amplitude than the brain waves. The magnetic component of the heart's field, which is around 100 times stronger than that produced by the brain . . . can be measured several feet away from the body.

- Rollin McCraty, Ph.D.

The reason our feelings are so magnetic is because feelings are stronger than thoughts. We get exactly what we want when we have positive feelings attached to that want. What we most deeply feel, we attract. That's why I needed to release the beliefs causing me to feel fat and unlovable before I could begin to make a slim, healthy body my new reality.

The outer purpose of our feelings is to create the life we want for ourselves. To attract more love, *feel* more love. To be joyful, *feel* joyful. To attract prosperity, act in ways that make you *feel* abundant. On the flip side, emotions like anger or frustration simply attract more things to annoy you. So focusing on Soul-affirming feelings that honour your spirit, combined with positive thought, is the best way to create the life you really want.

The inner purpose of our feelings is to keep us on path and purpose by connecting us to our truth. Positive feeling states are a sign that you're in sync with your Soul, while negative feelings are sure signs that you're out of sync.

Your feelings are guiding you. They are your compass. They point you in the right direction and light the way. And they give you real-time feedback. Feeling bad – upset, frustrated, powerless, angry? Take a moment to reassess and realign. Feeling good – happy, calm, blessed, abundant? Take note of how you are aligned and step even further in that direction.

So many people spend their whole lives resisting, shutting down, or turning away from their feelings. Which means they're missing out on the fool-proof guidance of their inbuilt compass – their feelings – to light the way.

This way of living doesn't mean that you never encounter negativity or suffering in your life. Think about those people in your life who are loving even when life offers up lemons, or generous despite being broke, or peaceful and calm even in crisis, or happily able to see the good in everything and everyone no matter the circumstance. There's a deep connectedness about such people. A real self-determination that sees them able to remain positive, even in the most negative of circumstances.

Such people have mastered the ability to differentiate between their thoughts, circumstances and feelings about themselves and their life.

In my own life, I may watch a programme and think that it is tragic, or horrible, or depressing, yet I'm still happy and in love with my life. I meet someone who seems overly fearful or negative about life, but I'm still connected to my sense of self within. Or I might have opinions about political issues or international events, but I can easily separate these from who I am and how I feel.

Our minds may make judgments, but the heart of you is constant. It's like that old adage, you can't always choose what happens to you, but you can always choose how you feel about it. Your feelings lead you back to who you really are. Your Soul.

Give yourself permission to feel

Your urges, your desires, your deepest feelings are how your Soul speaks to you. Honour those feelings, trust them and they will guide you true.

But sometimes feelings don't come easy. We are so used to tuning them out, that it becomes hard for us to 'read' them and understand what they're telling us.

Some of us are so disconnected from how we really feel that our lives become led by what we think. You hear of people saying they feel 'numb' after a particularly traumatic experience or tragic loss. We literally do have the ability to disconnect ourselves from our feelings. It's like an inbuilt protection mechanism. And sometimes it gets so familiar and comfortable that we think it's safer to keep that protection switched 'on' because it's easier than facing the reality of how we actually feel. So, repeated failed relationships may shut down your capacity to feel love and trust. A miscarriage may shut down your desires for motherhood. Bankruptcy may numb your feeling of being worthy to receive good things in life.

To feel, we first have to give ourselves permission to feel. Switch your feelings back on by asking yourself in any moment, *How do I really feel about this? Am I scared of feeling something about this?*

In this moment you may want to feel confident or clear. Radiant or resourceful. Peaceful and centred. Able to breathe. About yourself you may want to feel beautiful, or treasured, or awake, or sassy, or sensual or any number of deep, life-affirming things. And about life, you may want to feel oneness. Or secure. Or bountiful. Or joyful.

By having awareness of how you feel in the moment, you also consciously allow yourself to choose how to act. And when we can repeatedly choose actions that honour our spirit, we draw ever closer to Soul happiness.

Evoke your desired feelings through aligned choices. To feel treasured, make decisions that honour who you are and treasure every aspect of your being. You may choose to do one thing every day that treasures your inner self – from a pampering facial routine, to a centring yoga practice. To feel more sensual, you may choose to engage your senses through a massage, buying a new fragrance, or listening to music that lights you up.

The key is to know why you want to feel how you do. Your feelings are your true north and they will help you unlock the values that are part of your Soul code.

Let your values guide you

Values are our heart's deepest desires for our lives; our inner principles that guide and motivate us in our life. They are the things of utmost importance to us. The things we would never compromise. They govern our feelings, and determine the way we interact with and relate to the world, other people, and ourselves.

Our values are our hotline to our truest self. They just are. We don't decide them. They are already written as part of our Soul code for this life. They are an element of our being. Naturally embedded in who we are.

Values are how you desire to be. They are different to goals. Goals can be finite, achieved and ticked off. Values are enduring, inherent, inbuilt.

Let's use relationships as an example.

If it's important to you to be open and honest, that is a value and you will feel content, secure and settled when it is being expressed in your relationships. When it's not, your feelings will let you know.

If it is important to you to get married, that is a goal. Once you are married, the goal can be ticked off. To find the value, look deeper. If you want to get married, why is that? Perhaps you see marriage as a symbol of love or acceptance or unity. In which case, these deeper desires are actually your values. Marriage is just one expression of them.

Perhaps you are already clear on your values. Perfect. Living in tune with them will always guide you true.

If you find yourself wondering, *What exactly are my values?* Now's the time to start asking the inner questions and creating the space for the answers.

Deep down, what is really important to you? And why?

Why do you really want what you want?

What do you want to live for or stand for?

What qualities do you want to embody as a person?

What must you radiate in your life?

What would you never do?

Not everyone has the same values, and even if they did, they'd be expressed differently, in our own unique way. There is no right and wrong.

But, if you find it hard to answer these questions for yourself, look to others that you admire. What values do they live by? What do you appreciate about them? This will give you an insight into your own deeper values, because remember, we often see – and admire – in others what we fail to recognise in ourselves.

Values are your heart's deepest desires for how you want to *be*. They are not about what you want to get or do; they are about how you want to behave or act on an ongoing basis.

When you live in sync with your values, you open yourself to more peace, contentment and flow in your life. By living in tune with your values, you are being authentically you and life just flows.

Here is a short, by no means exhaustive, list of Soul values for the four key life areas. Use it to help you tune into your own values.

Purpose + Spirit

Essence, identity, spark, spirituality, intuition, inspiration, meaning, beliefs, faith, practices
- Acceptance: to accept myself, others and life with openness.
- Authenticity: to be true to myself.
- Beauty: to see, nurture and appreciate the beauty of myself, others, and the environment.
- Courage: to be daring, persistent, brave despite fear or difficulty.

- Freedom: to live freely and to have choice.
- Gratitude: to be thankful for myself, others and life.
- Love: to be love and share love and affection.
- Mindfulness: to be consciously aware and appreciative of every moment.
- Self-development: to keep evolving and living as the truest version of myself.
- Spirituality: to live with meaning and connect with something bigger than myself.

Lifestyle + Living

Home, belongings, work, business, money, education, learning, travel, entertainment, play

- Adventure: to allow myself experiences that feed my spirit.
- Challenge: to release all limits about what I can and cannot do.
- Curiosity: to explore and discover new opportunities and ways of being.
- Excitement: to feel engaged and stimulated in life and with how I spend my time.
- Industry: to be hard-working and dedicated.
- Creativity: to see new ways of doing things, to express myself creatively.
- Open-mindedness: to see the truth, think things through and see all points of view.
- Modesty: to be humble and let my achievements speak for themselves.
- Simplicity: to live an uncomplicated life of ease.
- Security: to be safe and protect myself and others, to be looked after and to have enough.

Love + Relationships

Love, romance, family, friendships, expression, giving, causes

- Contribution: to make a positive difference.

- Equality: to see everyone as equal and worthy.
- Forgiveness: to release hurts and be forgiving.
- Generosity: to be giving and generous of spirit.
- Honesty: to be sincere and truthful.
- Justice: to advocate justice and fairness.
- Kindness: to be caring, compassionate and nurturing.
- Respect: to be respectful, polite and considerate.
- Romance: to be romantic, affectionate, sensual and to express love.
- Trust: to be loyal, faithful, sincere, and reliable.

Health + Wellbeing

Body, fitness, nutrition, holistic self-care, healing, rest and relaxation, leisure, interests, hobbies

- Balance: to practice self-care and look after every aspect of myself.
- Fitness: to increase my physical stamina.
- Fun: to be fun-loving and playful.
- Humour: to laugh and see the lighter side of life.
- Independence: to do things my way.
- Nutrition: to nourish myself well and make healthy choices.
- Order: to have order, organisation and clarity in my life.
- Patience: to wait calmly for what I want.
- Peace: to feel inner-calm and serenity.
- Responsibility: to be responsible and accountable for my actions.

Reading over this list you may find that some values deeply resonate with you. They feel perfectly you. You may have thoughts and feelings about other values too. Or you may simply feel that you have no idea at all. And that's ok too. Trust that once you start asking the questions, you will get the answers. Allow yourself all the time you need.

Remember, understanding your values is simply about understanding how you most want to feel. And when you are really clear on that, you simply look a little deeper to see the values behind those desires.

You may feel a need for calm in your life. If you look a little deeper, the need to feel calm may be because peace (inner peace, peacefulness) is one of your core values. Or you may need to feel understood, because truth is a value. Or you may need to feel independent, because empowerment is a value. You may need to let go of fear because trust is a value. Or you need to let go of judgement, because acceptance is a value. Or you need to let go of indecision, because wisdom is a value. You get the idea.

Even if, until now, you have been unaware of your own Soul values, you will recall the times you have been living in-sync with them in your life. Because of how you felt. They were the times you felt calm, ordered and peaceful, when everything flowed and you felt connected to yourself and life.

Values give you a deeper clarity about yourself and your life. When you live in accordance with your values you are honouring your true self. Your values help you understand an aspect of your Soul purpose and part of your purpose is to embody your values in every part of your life.

✳

Simple reflection

This reflection time is designed to help you connect to your deepest feelings and desires. As always, use your journal or turn to the appropriate page in the Soul Happiness companion workbook.

Be self-full

Being self-full is important for giving your values permission to surface in your life. Help understand the dynamic between feeling selfish and selfless in your life right now, in order to create more self-full opportunities for yourself.

Complete the following sentences:

- I am my strongest, clearest me when…
- I love myself unconditionally because…
- I make time for myself in my life by…
- I give myself permission to be…
- When I say yes to… I say no to…

Say yes to your desired feelings

Your deepest feelings help you discover your values. Explore your feelings and desires for yourself and your life through the following questions.

- Right now I most want to feel… because…
- In my life I most want to feel… because…
- About myself I most want to feel… because…

Tune into your values

Your values are what you stand for, and they are a key aspect of your Soul code. Unlocking them ensures you are more able to be authentically you and align with your inner and outer purpose. So, for example, if you want to have a successful career, the value might be success, or security, or independence, or recognition. Everyone's desires are different. Why you want something will be totally different to the motivators for someone else.

- Answer your deepest questions:

  - The qualities I most want to embody are... because...

  - In the world, I most want to radiate... because...

  - I will never... because...

  - My best possible life is one of...

- Write as many answers as you have to these questions. Then summarise your answers into one or two words based on why it is important to you.

- Add to the list of words you have with values that resonate with you from the list on pages 55-57 or other values that come to mind.

- Review your list. Group similar values together. For example, if you had values like compassion, giving and caring, you could group them together as 'kindness'. Aim to create a list of 12 core values, three in each key area of your life: purpose + spirit, lifestyle + living, love + relationships, health + wellbeing.

- Another way to determine your values is to work through the list on pages 55-57, putting an A beside those values that are absolutely important to you, a B beside the next most important values and so on. Until you have a list of 12 core values.

- When you have done this exercise, write your values somewhere special. They are what you stand for.

Simple promise

Make this simple promise to yourself now. Remind yourself of this promise throughout your day or write it down where you will see it.

I see my truth and honour how I feel. Always.

Simple practices

These simple steps can help you put the ideas in this chapter into practice. Remember, there is power in doing something. Anything. Just one thing. Because the moment you do, you make a conscious change in your life.

Be present with your feelings. Give your fullest attention to whatever the moment presents. Ask yourself, *How do I really feel about this?*

Be more of how you want to feel. Make a choice to do more of the things that align with how you most want to feel in your life. You open yourself up to greater happiness and contentment that way.

Keep positive. Separate your thoughts from your feelings. Try watching the news and separate the thoughts you may have about stories or events from the way you feel about yourself and your life.

Let yourself be. For a moment allow yourself to drop everything. Once a day, for a moment. Or once a week for a day. Or once a month for a week. Do what feels right. Give your true self the space to expand.

Listen to your needs. Allow yourself to be important. Put yourself first. Commit to self-full acts that feed your spirit.

Release something. Choose one thing. One fear. One aspect of self-doubt. Perhaps even something you are avoiding. If it doesn't serve you, choose to let it go.

Take note of others. Who do you admire? Often those people, or the work they do and the things you admire them for, are the perfect pointers to your deepest truth.

CHAPTER 5

secret 5: gifts are for sharing

I am capable of what every other human is capable of.
~ Maya Angelou

Because our Soul purpose is about being rather than doing, you only discover it when you know yourself completely. When you know who you are, what you love, what makes you special, you can more fully be who you truly are.

The Temple of Apollo at Delphi, a Greek site of ancient wisdom that I was blessed to visit, is engraved with the words "know thyself". In other words, to live a purposeful life, know what you value, what you love, how you want to be, and what your innate gifts and strengths are.

And so this chapter focuses on helping you unlock the next aspect of your Soul code, your Soul character. Who we are drives what we do, and Soul character is your essence. It is defined by your gifts, strengths and passions.

To connect with your character, you have to be able to see what is special and unique about yourself. And, more than that, you need to be able to positively express those qualities in your life.

Just as Soul values are innate, so are your Soul gifts. They are deeply a part of who you are, and living your life in tune with your gifts and passions allows you to feel filled up. It's literally like saying 'Yes' to who you really are in every moment.

I started to realise my own unique Soul gifts when I took a deeper view of my own perceived weaknesses.

I used to think it was a weakness to be sensitive. I used to take everything to heart. Sense the true meaning behind spoken words. Physically feel the energy behind arguments. But you know what? Sensitivity is a gift. Now I understand it more, I can manifest it more positively in my life to help people. Being extra sensitive also means you become super resilient. Which is also a gift.

I used to think it was a weakness to like being by myself. Even now I love my own company. But in my younger years I would spend endless hours by myself, entertaining myself, content to be with myself. Now it is in my own company that my ideas develop and I write. My own company allows me to be focused and clear, which are also gifts.

I used to think it was a weakness to need structure. I need lists. I need to know the big picture. I need to know where we're going and how we'll get there. I know the detail will take care of itself, but I do feel more comfortable if the big pieces of the puzzle are in place. Yet some people can breeze through life being spontaneous and making sudden turns in the blink of an eye. I wanted to be like that for so long, yet every time I tried to I would feel incredibly uncomfortable. Yet this weakness is the insight to perhaps one of my most unique gifts. I have an uncanny ability to order, structure and make sense of information. I can quickly and logically break things down into steps and stages, because my mind likes to work in 'chunks' of information. I'm also extremely practical. All great talents to have, especially when it comes to writing books.

I used to think it was a weakness to want to fix things. I used to feel like it was my responsibility to fix everything. I'm always the person with the suggestion of how to make things better. Always thinking there must be a better way. Some people probably find that annoying, because I can always see what needs to be done. You know those situations where a friend is outpouring grief, heartache and overwhelm, yet it feels like you have complete crystal clear clarity about what she needs to do to get her life back on track? That's me. Now I know that kind of clarity and insight is a gift, and one that I use every day in my work as a coach and healer.

I used to think it was a weakness to like to be in charge. Maybe it's an eldest child thing, but I usually just take charge. I'm the one that organises things. Buys the group birthday present. Sets the plan for the year. Organises the holiday. Show me what needs to be done, give me a job and I'll do it. But I want to do it my way. You know what the gift is in that? I am an individual and I am confident to set a direction and follow through on it. Nearly always unwaveringly. Take this book for example. I'm doing it my way. I'm sharing my own vision. It's about being uniquely me, and sharing what I know in my own way to help you. The only person I need to be answerable to for that is me.

Really, if I look at it, all the things that I've been told weren't so great about me, or that I needed to work on or improve, were actually hiding the innate gifts I needed to harness in my life. They were also hiding lessons too. The same will be true for you too. The gifts that are most closely aligned to your Soul purpose will be disguised or hidden under the things that you have been told, or that you yourself think, are your biggest weaknesses.

Look within

The qualities we need to live a life with purpose have been with us since childhood too. Not only does your childhood reveal your interests, it reveals your innate qualities and gifts. These are the things that are inherently part of you. More than your personality, they define your spirit. It is our spirit that brings us life, colour, personality, traits, likes, dislikes, and more. Our spirit is who we are, here and now.

In *Beyond Happiness,* I talked about your 'gifts basket' and wrote:

> *We have been given everything we need to create magic in our lives. Yet we don't often see our gifts.*

Without self-love, it is often impossible to open yourself up to your gifts or to see and accept that you have them. But sometimes they will present themselves as an underlying theme in your life. We are all born with a set of amazing gifts. We unconsciously weave these into our days. You may be an eternal optimist, you may have a knack for always knowing the right thing to say, or you may have a great eye for detail. Instead of being down on yourself for things you could have done differently or better, see your gifts.

We play down our innate gifts and talents because we lack self-worth and self-love and because we contain our light. We often take things about ourselves for granted. We assume that everyone is like us, that we're not so distinctively special at all. We often fail to recognise our unique talents, our special strengths. These virtues link intrinsically with your Soul purpose. Recognising them connects you more strongly to your true self. Be grateful for yourself and all your amazing gifts.

But when it comes to thinking about – or even trying to name – our gifts, we suddenly find it hard to articulate the things that define who we really are. Sometimes we even confuse the difference between behaviours and gifts.

Behaviours are the outward expression of what really lies within. Behaviours can usually be modified. The behaviours you most identify with for yourself are not necessarily your gifts, unless, those behaviours consistently infuse every part of your life. In other words, if you're like that all the time.

Behaviours are essentially how we adapt to the environment around us. There may be the 'work' you. The 'best friend' you. The 'parental' you. The 'fun' you. The 'serious' you.

The 'work' you may be patient, calm and unflappable in the office. Yet you may find these behaviours aren't reflected in the 'home' you. You may be overwhelmed, unorganised and prone to erupting at those you love.

We have become so good at modifying our behaviour depending on the circumstance, the activity or the people we're with. These are just simply learned patterns of behaviour, and if you look deeply at what lies beneath, these patterns are heavily influenced by our life layers. We create these behaviours based on how we think we have to be.

Gifts, however, are inherent, often lying dormant, and yearning to be released. Your true gifts are waiting to be recognised.

For example, take the word 'friendly'. You may think that is a nice gift. Everyone wants to be perceived as open, approachable and friendly, right? But stop to consider that being naturally friendly in some situations is actually just one form of expression of a much deeper gift. An open heart and an openness to accepting others.

Or we may think of ourselves as 'organised' or 'focused'. Again, we may be tuning more into our surface behaviours. Most of us could choose to be more or less organised or focused depending on the situation or who we are with. But our true gifts lie much deeper than this. Perhaps the underlying gift that creates organised behaviour is clear insight with the ability to visualise a flow of events.

Our feelings not only link us to our values, they link us to our gifts. You may want to feel calm because you possess a calming energy. You may want to feel empowered, because you have the gift of empowering others. You may desire insight because you are ignoring your own higher awareness. You may want to feel understood because you have the special gift of seeing the truth of others. So look carefully at how you wish to feel. It is a large pointer to your inner gifts.

Believe you are special

Here's the thing. No matter what you've been told, how much you think you need to change, or how many weaknesses you're convinced you have, the reality couldn't be further from the truth. Perhaps there are things you need to learn, yes. Different choices you need to make, sure. But your Soul code ensures you are perfect in every way to be uniquely you and to fulfil your Soul purpose.

You have special, unique gifts that, when blended with your passions, experiences and values, creates something that only you have. And there is a place in the world for that something that only you can perfectly bring. It is your essence that brings your gifts to life.

Our gifts and talents are usually such a part of who we are that often we don't see them. We take them for granted. Or we assume that everyone else is like us, thinks like us, sees the world like us. But this is simply not the case.

Take me for example. Yes, someone else might be a writer too, a good one. And they may even author books on themes similar to those I write about. So in essence, we share some similar talents and gifts, possibly values, and even the same interests in subject matter. But, it is my other gifts, the essence of me, my experiences, my way of looking at and processing information, my own unique 'voice' or the way I like to write that makes me unique. And I know there are people who need to hear what I have to say, how I have to say it.

You may think we are all the same. But we most definitely are not. You are beautifully, incomparably, unique. Exactly as you're meant to be.

Be multi-passionate

Our passions go hand in hand with our Soul gifts. Passions are an inherent part of our Soul character. Passions are what drive you, what energise you, what make you want to jump out of bed in the morning. Simply put, your passions are your deepest loves.

What do you truly love? What do you adore? What lights you up? What excites you?

The things you are deeply passionate about will be completely different to the person sitting across the desk from you, your friends, your siblings, or even your children.

I love fresh flowers, colour, and symmetry. I'm passionate about gorgeous looking spaces and gardens. I treasure beautiful things. I adore order and simplicity. It is this passion that I inject into my work too. These passions are reflected in my inner and my outer life.

Our passions can be many, and multi-layered. Let's call it multi-passionate. I certainly am, and I bet you are too.

Somewhere along the way, most people pick up the idea that we should choose one thing that becomes our special life focus, and let go of everything else that may interest us. Having one passion is the 'correct' way to live – we can't indulge all our passions, and we most certainly can't do more than one thing at a time. Or so we've been told. But if you dedicate all your time to just one thing, what happens to everything else?

In decades past, you didn't choose a career, *it* chose you. Any job was a good job. Choices were based on earning potential rather than fulfilment. And when you got a job, you had it for life. But those days are gone.

Today, in the western world, we are blessed beyond belief with self-determination and the choice to be and do anything our heart desires. We have the freedom to change direction, to make new choices, and to create different results.

So many of us find ourselves straddling this chasm between the old beliefs and the new reality. It's now so common for people to embark on 'realistic', 'sensible', 'well chosen' career paths, only to realise years – even decades – later that it wasn't the right path. That something is missing. But what's really interesting is that faced with this scenario, so many of us are choosing to indulge our many passions, instead of just selecting a different, singular one. We have multiple business interests, or portfolios, or careers and we love it. This kind of approach really allows us to feed our spirit.

Take me for example. I left my upsized career, initially to set up my own energy practice. But all the new space and freedom in my life helped me quickly see I could also indulge my other passions as well. I gave myself permission to become multi-passionate. Writing, coaching, designing, healing, Soulful living. I wanted to do it all. And so I did. I became a life coach. I started writing. I indulged my love of artistic expression by taking charge of the design and layout of all my online material and books.

All of it served to fill me up in a beautiful, nourishing way. And it still does. It feeds my free-spirited side, it lets me taste and experience different things, it lets me explore the multidimensional nature of who I am. And I love it.

You don't have to just choose one thing either. You can choose to honour everything you love and that you're passionate about. On some level, you've already worked out how all your gorgeous talents and abilities will weave together. The key is to just start somewhere. Why can't you be a lawyer by day, jazz musician by night, culinary tapas genius at home, and Master's squash champion in your spare time? Do what you love, the opportunities will come.

When you recognise that you have more than one passion and you allow yourself to indulge as many of your loves as you can, life begins to flow. That's what unlocking your Soul character is all about.

Do what you love today

Usually we feel unfulfilled in our lives because we aren't honouring our passions and our gifts. We aren't being who we really are, or doing the things that bring us joy. Even if you don't know what your purpose is, the easiest place to start is to identify your passions and your gifts and then start weaving them into your life. Even if this means just doing one thing that you love each day.

Doing what you love doesn't mean you need to make a radical lifestyle change straight away. Right now, you can simply choose to take gradual steps to weave more of what you love into your life. Start small, start today, or start tomorrow. Just start. You don't have to quit your job. You can spend a few hours a day, or even just a few hours a week doing what you love.

When you do that, you're changing your vibration. Doing what we love literally lights us up.

Maybe you love photography and being creative. Instead of quitting your job, you could start taking the 'official' photos at your current workplace. Or helping out as a studio assistant in your spare time. Or setting up your own side business as a portrait photographer. Enter competitions. Join clubs. Set up a Facebook page to share your images. Whatever you do, you'll be shifting your energy and more ideas and opportunities that support that new vibe you're putting out will come along. And as long as you are open to the opportunities, and you allow them in, who knows where it will lead. Eventually you could have your own successful photography business, or become a photography tutor, or more. You may not see how that might happen right now, but it will, if you allow it to.

Don't limit your views about which passion to follow by what you think you can make the most money doing. If you stop to think – and perhaps do some research – you will see that there are people in the world, right now, making money doing exactly what you'd love to do. Quite simply, with the right attitude, an open mind, and the willingness to try, even the most unusual of passions can become part of a nourishing, supportive career.

So start living your passions, your loves, your dreams, your desires. Share your gifts. You already know exactly what you'd love to be doing. And you've dismissed it a thousand times already. Enough of the dismissing. Start being who you really are today. Start small. Just start.

The 12 Soul gifts

We all have many different things that we are good at. The things that seem to just come naturally to us where others may struggle. But there's a difference between everyday gifts and Soul gifts.

Soul gifts are what we are here to share in the world. We do this through our outer purpose. We choose them as part of our Soul code before we incarnate. Our gifts can be strongly aligned to our values, and they often become the outer expression of our inner self.

Remember, when you master a lesson you become a teacher. As a teacher you share your Soul gifts in order to help others. But sometimes we fail to recognise our own beauty and fail to see – let alone accept – our gifts. Our treasures remain locked within us, and that is when Soul gifts become our inner challenges. As challenges, they are teaching us to accept our true self and embrace our inner purpose.

There are 12 Soul gifts. When we fully embrace our inner gifts we can harness them to fulfil our outer purpose. You can either embrace your gifts, or suppress them. When you embrace them, you will notice that you share this gift in some part of your life. When you suppress a gift, you will notice you experience challenges related to it.

The 12 Soul gifts are:

To protect
- These people love creating solid foundations for themselves and others. Security and safety are important. They feel responsible for the care and protection of others, their community, animals and the planet.
- People suppressing this gift often have an unhealthy relationship with money, can tend to be over-protective and worrying.

To nurture
- These people often take on selfless roles. They love supporting, caring for and looking after others. They thrive on helping others to shine, often creating the environment to do so. Always thoughtful, they get immense satisfaction from seeing others happy.
- People suppressing this gift can tend to find it hard to say yes to their needs, look after themselves, ask for help, or know what they want in their own lives. They can often have boundary issues, opening themselves up to people taking more and more.

To organise

- These people love structure and lists. They see the big picture and know the steps to get there. They harness people and resources well, and are at home leading or managing projects. They are the goal-oriented doers who get things done.
- People suppressing this gift can get overwhelmed easily yet find it hard to delegate. They may be surrounded with mental and physical clutter. They can be fixated on their way of doing things and find it hard to be flexible.

To love

- These people give love and compassion unconditionally. Gentle, peaceful spirits, they are patient with themselves and others. They see the beauty of all beings, and show others how to love themselves and to awaken their heart's truth.
- People suppressing this gift are deeply critical of themselves, often feeling as though they are unworthy of love and good things in their lives. They are scared of being hurt or judged, and often feel disconnected from themselves.

To communicate

- These people love sharing information, ideas and wisdom. They feel compelled to speak the truth and they uplift and inspire others with new ways of thinking and being. They are the 'how to' people, and are good at explaining and packaging information and instructions.
- People suppressing this gift often have difficulty expressing their emotion, sharing opinions or standing firm on a belief, yet find it easy to engage in meaningless chatter. They base their own ideals, beliefs and values on others.

To teach

- These people really cannot help but teach and guide others, and get satisfaction from helping others grow. They love ideas and sparking new connections. They love learning, and immediately want to

share information and discoveries with others.
- People suppressing this gift can be opinionated with narrow views. They have a need to be right and can find it difficult to accept other's points of views. They can feel stupid and become frustrated if they do not know how to do something.

To heal
- These people love harmony and often have a calm peaceful energy. Their presence alone is sometimes enough to soothe or reconcile situations. They are highly sensitive, and are drawn to help others heal in a physical, mental, emotional or spiritual way.
- People suppressing this gift may find themselves attracting friends and partners who are wounded or need 'fixing'. They have a need to constantly improve other people's lives. They can easily feel at the point of emotional overload and have frequent outbursts

To lead
- These people love to dream big. They are comfortable being centre stage. They are trailblazers with the courage to break moulds and forge new paths. They relentlessly pursue their goals and put their name or their mark to the things they achieve. They excel at motivating others, and preserving harmony with groups.
- People suppressing this gift often feel different, but lack the courage to be different. They may shun responsibility, feel superior to others, and dislike being told what to do.

To create
- These people love to ask "What if?" They are the searchers, the seekers, the inventors, the optimists, the creators who show us new possibilities. They find new ways of doing things, navigate problems with ease, and bring new inspiration into the world.
- People suppressing this gift often need to follow instructions to the letter, even in a recipe. They may be unmoved by beauty, even that of a flower. They may look to others for ideas and direction, or have difficulty bringing their ideas into being.

To empower
- These people are natural inspirers and coaches who motivate others to be their best. They see that our potential is only limited by our belief, and they show others how to reach their full potential in life. They believe in the infinite possibilities of life, and empower others to do the same.
- People suppressing this gift are often oblivious to their own talents and abilities. They feel down-trodden, dictated to and unable to be self-determining in their life. They often feel like they are not in charge and disempower themselves through indecisiveness, overeating and addictive behaviour.

To awaken
- These people are here to open our minds to a new way of being, and to connect us to our own spiritual gifts. They show us the interconnectedness of all, and how to access our higher consciousness, intuition and wisdom.
- People suppressing this gift usually interpret the actions of others in a negative way, or have negative patterns continually surfacing in their lives. They can be judgemental and have difficultly trusting other people, and themselves.

To transform
- These people are fearless catalysts for change on a personal, social and most often world stage. They believe one person can make a difference and they are guiding us to wake up. They are peaceful warriors who believe in the good of all. They have ceaseless energy for the causes they passionately believe in. They don't just think, they do.
- People suppressing this gift often anger quickly but feel powerless. They feel irritated easily, and are quick to see injustice. They can find themselves out of alignment with others, including friends, colleagues or employers, and compromise their true values for the sake of harmony.

Most often, people will have four main gifts. Two they have mastered and that link strongly to their outer purpose, one that is an inner gift to accept, and one that is a dormant gift and therefore manifesting as a significant challenge in their life.

But it is not unusual for people to be expressing all 12 gifts to varying degrees. Some gifts you may have been honing all your life, others will feel less natural to you, but they are all part of our whole. They are all interdependent. And each will build on the other. You will likely find that when you have said yes to the inner aspect of your gift, it becomes fully available for you to express in your outer life. The more you open to your gifts, and see how your essence makes your expression of it unique, the more you unlock them.

For example, if you feel guided to serve female entrepreneurs by providing them with the processes to streamline their business practice, you may be using the gift of organisation. When you then feel guided to create your own signature toolkit and training programme, you move into creating. When you set up your own magazine, you expand into communication and teaching. When you establish an international network, your gift of leadership comes to the fore. And so on. This is also an example of how there is an endless synergy between your openness to grow and move forward on your life purpose, and the harnessing of your gifts to ensure an easy flow.

You may think just 12 Soul gifts for everyone on earth seems quite narrow. But think of it this way. When I was growing up I played the piano. I remember being intrigued that the musical scale only had seven notes. Just seven. Yet there were hundreds of sheets of music haphazardly stacked on top of the piano in the corner of our dining room. Every one created from just seven notes. There have been untold pieces of music created in the world throughout time, each beautiful, moving, even inspiring in its own way. Your gifts are the same. You make them unique because you are you. And it is up to you to share your beautiful song with the world.

Simple reflection

To bring more of your inner self into the world, you need to align your gifts and passions. This reflection will help you really explore your special gifts and talents as a step towards understanding how you may express them in the world.

It can be hard to focus on our positive qualities, so take time, and be completely honest with yourself.

As always, turn to a fresh page in your journal or the relevant page in the Soul Happiness companion workbook.

Natural gifts

- Take time to reflect on and answer the following questions.
  - I am really good at all these things…
  - I've always thought of… as a weakness, but really it's hiding my gift of…
  - My best skill or ability is…
  - The thing people most value or appreciate about me is…

- Distil your answers to all these questions into single words, and write them on a fresh page in your journal titled MY GIFTS.

- Keep adding to this page with words that represent the natural talents and abilities you have. All the things you're amazing at. It's okay to blow your own trumpet!

- For each, ask yourself: Is there an even deeper gift underneath the one I have already seen? What does this gift really say about me? How am I using it or expressing it in my world?

- Put circles around, or highlight, those you consider your highest, most innate gifts.

True passions

- To discover your passions, ask yourself:
  - What do I truly love?
  - What do I adore?
  - What lights me up?
  - What excites me?
  - What would I spend my time doing if I had $10 million?

- Draw two columns on a fresh page in your journal titled MY PASSIONS. Write your answers to these questions in the left hand column. Note every new point on a new line.

- For every passion or love in your left hand column, in the right hand column write an idea for how you can do more, or experience more of it in your life.

- You may like to make it actionable by adding timeframes as well.

Soul gifts

- Revisit the Soul gifts on pages 72-75. Start a new page in your journal titled MY SOUL GIFTS, and answer these questions.
  - Which gifts resonate with you most? Why is that?
  - How are you expressing these gifts now?
  - Which gifts do you feel you may be suppressing and what challenges are you aware of in your life relating to them?

- You may wish to go a step further, revisiting this page in the weeks, months and even years to come, adding to it and even choosing what you consider your top gifts. When you recognise your gifts, your true self will start bringing you guidance as to what to do with them and how they match with your Soul purpose.

Simple promise

Make this simple promise to yourself now. Remind yourself of this promise throughout your day or write it down where you will see it.

I shine my light and allow my inner and outer worlds to align.

Simple practices

These simple steps can help you put the ideas in this chapter into practice. Remember, there is power in doing something. Anything. Just one thing. Because the moment you do, you make a conscious change in your life.

Do it for love. Don't limit your views about what you love, or what you think your outer purpose is, by what you think you can make a lot of money doing. When you do things from love, abundance follows.

Learn. Fill your life with your passions. Read books on topics that interest you. Take night classes to learn a new skill. Join a special interest group. Volunteer your time.

Look deeper. What's the most common gift or trait you notice in others? The thing that leaves you thinking, *Why is everyone good at that except me?* Remember, we see in others what we cannot see in ourselves. That thing will very likely be one of your core gifts.

Speak up. Consider how you can weave your passions into your current work. Ask to head a project on a topic you're interested in. Talk to your boss about trying your hand at something new. Seek training in an area that interests you.

Start now. Choose one of your passions or loves and decide to start it, do more of it, say yes to it, now.

Release perception. We can shut down our gifts, and limit our talents because we think others are better than us at the same thing. Know you are unique and allow all of you to shine.

♡

simple meditation

Shine Brightly

Get comfortable in your meditation space.

Breathe in through your nose and out through your mouth.

Breathe deeply and feel all tension leave you. Relax.

Draw in divine love and light.

Feel love infuse your cells, your heart, your being.

Gently release all self-doubt. All self-limitation.

See yourself with a loving heart. Fill yourself with light.

Know your deepest truth. See yourself anew.

You are perfect. You are special. You are loved.

Embrace your true power. Your boundless potential.

Allow your essence, the brilliance of you to shine.

Say 'Yes' to your true beauty. Express all that you are.

You glow like the sun and encircle the world.

Uniquely. Lovingly. Perfectly.

And so it is.

CHAPTER 6

secret 6: you are the path

You cannot travel the path until you have become the path itself.
~ Buddha

This chapter is about unlocking the last aspect of your Soul code, your Soul path. Much like any path, there will be markers or landmarks along the way. Sometimes they appear as giant sign posts, other times as tiny breadcrumbs, but they all point to a deeper understanding of who you are. You simply have to know how to spot them. This chapter will show you where to look.

Now, when I look back on my life, I sometimes wonder why it took me so long to get here. It is so in-my-face obvious that I would end up right here – as an author, a creator, an inspirer, a healer, an intuitive. I want to say that the answers were there all along, but it's actually that the *real me* – my true self, my spirit, my essence – was there all along. More often than not, drowned out or overshadowed by life.

Regardless of how long it took me to wake up to them, there were so many signs that appeared along my path. I have so many childhood memories, so many teenage recollections, all of which have taken on a new meaning now that I look back with the gift of hindsight.

As a child I used to love playing teacher. I would line up my dolls and teddy bears on my bedroom floor and read to them, or teach from a book, or just talk about whatever I wanted to. I liked being at the front and I didn't like playing so much if I couldn't be the teacher, or the driver of our imaginary bus, or the judge of our lounge room talent competition. I always loved reading and books, racing ahead of the 'standard' reading age as a child, and devouring my favourite books over and over again.

I loved to write, taking great pride in the creative visual presentation of my school projects, and later my essays and assignments. I remember in my early teens being thrilled to have the exclusive use of my Mum's dusty old typewriter. I set it up on the desk in my room, shut myself away from the rest of the family and spent hours typing away. I loved the click clack of the keys and seeing my words in print on the paper. I think many a secondary school English assignment came through that old typewriter. Interestingly, at school I was never particularly recognised for my writing ability. But I loved writing anyway and always fancied myself as an author, although it seemed far too difficult and unrealistic.

Instead I pursued a career in public relations and marketing. It was either that or journalism, but I was drawn to the more creative aspects of marketing. While studying for my degree, I bought my first computer. It was a whole new world of creative expression for me! I spent absolutely hours typing away on that beloved computer.

By this time in my life, my late teens, I had become deeply interested in the lives of inspirational people and in exploring spirituality. These themes were reflected in the books that I devoured so eagerly. I dived headfirst into books about the spiritual traditions of people like the Native American Indians. I was fascinated by Nelson Mandela's book *Long Walk to Freedom*, and was mesmerised at the thought of someone being treated so very unjustly for so long, yet still maintaining a sense of self-belief, integrity, kindness and the ability to change a country (and the world). To me that was magic. Similarly, I was intrigued by stories of people like Helen Keller, Leonardo Da Vinci and more. I felt so inspired by their lives, by their deeply prophetic insight and their clarity of purpose. I loved who they were, what they stood for, and their timeless words of wisdom. I think somewhere inside I knew I wanted to be like that. I wanted to inspire others.

In my early 20s, I went through a phase of making my own inspirational books. They were filled with whatever quotes and nuggets of wisdom resonated with me at the time, and I'd give them away to the people around me. I distinctly remember one I made for my brother to inspire him during a tough time. It was the size of a business envelope, with a cover made out of heavy card covered in a deep purple textured paper. I made a plaster-cast heart, which I painted gold, to stick on the cover. I used my new computer to design and layout the inside pages, using handpicked quotes to let my brother know that I saw those words in him. I remember perfectly trimming those pages, inserting them into the covers, and securing everything together with gold push-pin studs. I was so proud of that book. The act of creation was immensely fulfilling and that book was awesome.

I used to love making things for other people – books, birthday and Christmas cards, bookmarks and other creative projects. They all honed my creative juices, and also my ability to conceptualise something and then bring it to life. I used to call them 'Marnie Creations', and I'd put a little stamp on the back. I guess even this book you hold in your hands is a Marnie Creation!

While studying for my degree I had my first words appear in print, as the columnist for the student newspaper. My column was called 'Such is Life', and it was all about how to accept the ups and downs of life. Although it had a light-hearted slant, my 19-year-old self was clearly laying the groundwork for things to come!

These were all inborn. No one pushed me in that direction, it all came from within. An organic, natural progression.

But that isn't to say I wasn't also influenced by the intricacies of life. I was. And it caused me to develop a rather hefty stack of life layers by my late 20s. Even though my true self showed itself at times, the older I got the more I got caught up in the deeply programmed belief systems I had, and the less I wrote and created from a place of joy.

I was thrown in the deep end in my first job as a sole-charge communication manager – at 21 – freaking out on the inside, and pushing myself unbelievably hard to prove to everyone that I could do it. At the time I was possibly the youngest person in such a sole position in my industry. It was intense, but again, I was leading, paving the way, calling the shots, making the decisions, only this time there was more than my dolls and teddies and younger siblings involved. Inevitably the more responsibility I had, the harder I worked, the more I felt I needed to prove, and the more I got sucked into the 'career' trap... and the further and further I moved away from who I really was.

I've described what happened from there in *Beyond Happiness*. A house fire in my late 20s was a really big course-correcting moment for me. As were the experiences that followed. And the further into my 30s I got, the more I asked the same Soul-searching questions that we're diving into in this book – *Who am I? What is it all about? What am I here for?* I believe that once you ask the questions you always get an answer. And so, for me, little by little my life changed and little by little I stepped closer back to the true me.

It's only in the process of writing this book that I have recalled some of these early life experiences. But even in doing so, it's no wonder I am here right now. An author sharing my own lived wisdom, and an inspirer creating tools and programmes to teach and help others. I love it. And I love how the trail of breadcrumbs was there all along, if only I had paused to see it sooner.

Our past truly does hold the keys to our purpose.

You already know

Despite what may be running through your mind right now, connecting to your purpose is not difficult at all. In fact, it's easy when you know how. You have already ensured you have all the tools you need for this life and your purpose. And you have also left yourself a trail of breadcrumbs along the way, leading you back to who you really are and what you have intended for yourself in this life. The thing you most need to do is create space and give yourself time.

Look at it like this. I've got a home handy toolkit. The kind that comes in a case, and when you open it, it has a place for every tool. When everything is in the correct place, the tools fit perfectly and securely into the space created for them.

You have created your own toolkit for life too. Every toolkit has a range of tools, some are the same for everyone, and others are unique only to you. Along the way you've picked up some things that may not fit perfectly and securely into your toolkit. Things like our beliefs, which can which can be hardwired from childhood and not resonate with who we truly are. That's like trying to fit the hammer in the space meant for the screwdriver.

We already know, on some level of our being, what we are here for. And we have come prepared with all the tools we need. We have already unlocked several pieces of your Soul code in previous chapters – your Soul lessons, Soul values and Soul gifts.

In this chapter we will look at all the aspects of your life path pointing to your purpose in life:

- Your family circumstances and your childhood. Family is our first point of learning and Souls choose a family based on the learning opportunities they offer.
- The energetic influences of the astrological and numerological configurations present at the time of your birth.
- The signs and the synchronicities that have been dotted throughout your life.

Everything you need, whether it be for yourself, for life, for happiness and contentment – and most certainly for your purpose – is already within you. It's time to look at your history with fresh eyes and to see the not-so-hidden meanings.

The first true you

Many of us fail to see what is within us, because we rely only on our conscious mind for answers. The older we become, the more we tend to distance ourselves from our inner truth.

Children are undeniably in tune with their spirits. When you are born, you and your true self are as one, and you vibrate most closely to your Soul-self until around the age of two to three, when the existing you and the true you start to separate.

The older we get the more life hides our true nature from us. We quickly learn to mould ourselves into someone we're not in order to fulfil other people's views of the 'perfect' child we should be. When we hear 'don't' and 'won't' and 'can't' and 'stop' and 'no' and limiting words such as this, it creates an invisible barrier or box around us. Until we are around the age of seven, our true self tries to step out of this barrier every now and then, yet any limiting response we receive sends us quickly back. This is how we become even more separated from who we truly are, and how we end up living our life shaped entirely by other people's beliefs and perceptions about who we should be. We form false beliefs about ourselves and our lives.

Ironically, it is around the age of two to three, when this separation starts, that is generally known in parenting circles as the 'terrible twos'. What is really happening is that the spirit is protesting at the separation from itself.

Even at a young age our innate gifts and talents are trying to make themselves known. Your life purpose would have been expressed through the games you played, the art you made, the fantasy worlds you created, and the activities you most enjoyed in those younger years. I think if we all took the time to look back on our childhood we would see the foundations of our future path in the making.

This is evident when we look at the childhood genius of some of our modern figureheads. Filmmaker Steven Spielberg was ingeniously creative even as a child. Apparently he made a plastic skull with a red light shining through the eye sockets and used it to scare his sisters by hiding it in a closet. It became the basis for one of the scenes in his classic scary movie, Poltergeist. And when Donald Trump was a boy, he borrowed his brother's building blocks, built a masterpiece structure, and then glued the blocks together. A sign of his future property magnate-self, no doubt.

The fact is our childhoods and early lives contain the clues for the intentions we carried into this life – for who we are, what we are here to do, and the challenges we will face. Sometimes it's downright obvious, like the two previous examples, or even my own story (even though it wasn't obvious to me until the process of writing this book!). Other times, perhaps the memories aren't so forthcoming or the clues are not so clear.

Just persevere. Your reason for being here is already inside of you – you simply need to access the information. I believe your purpose has always been with you, and it is most likely locked away in your childhood memories. That's why paying attention to those long-ago recollections is one of the easiest places to start looking.

Our childhood passions reveal our genuine selves, as opposed to the person we become after life wraps its layers around our beautiful little spirits. So travel back to the first you, the true you, and I'll bet you'll see her or him standing there ready to give you all the answers you seek.

It is also worthwhile to look closely at the tendencies you had as a child that have especially stuck with you. They might be telling you something very important about who you are and who you are meant to be. Did you create a grand Barbie mansion, and later become an interior designer? Did you adore flowers, and later become a florist or landscape designer? Did you have a knack for repairing the chain when it came off your bike, and later became an engineer or mechanic? What we often dismiss as child's play can actually be clues to our future occupation or purpose.

We can also learn a lot about ourselves by diving deep into our early family life. There will be as many insights there as you take the time to mine for. What was your family dynamic like when you were growing up? Were there set roles and responsibilities? Was money tight? How much freedom do you feel you had?

Birth order is important too. How many siblings do you have? Where do you fall in the birth order? Eldest children are generally strong, introverted, practical, loyal, creative and good leaders. Second children are generally determined, competitive, expressive, and able to set and fulfil goals. Third children are generally clever, talkative, co-operative, fair, good negotiators. And so on.

What traits or qualities have you learned from your parents and your grandparents? Were there beliefs that infused your whole family, like these from my family; "money doesn't grow on trees", and "children should be seen and not heard". Are there enduring family beliefs or attitudes that go back several generations? "You have to work hard to get anywhere in life," was a firm belief in my family.

Our families are our first teachers. We learn about giving and receiving, about unconditional love, about sharing, and about contributing to others. It is worthwhile to also look at how your family life may have shaped your beliefs, behaviour and choices as you grew into adulthood.

The secrets of the stars

There are also energetically encoded signs specific to us, that hold information and insights about who we are, our gifts and even our purpose in life.

Vibrational patterns like astrology and numerology can impact our lives. Everything has a vibration, and the more in tune you are with the vibrations that influence you, including planetary alignment and numerological patterns, the more harmony and flow you will experience in your life.

Now I am not an expert in either astrology or numerology. But it has been fascinating in my own life to draw the comparisons between the information these tools provide and my own purpose. For that reason I share my basic knowledge here, and if it intrigues you as much as it does me, I encourage you to explore these aspects further for yourself.

Astrology

Astrology is a tool based on planetary configurations at the time of our birth. The energy of these configurations is said to influence us, even down to our strengths, gifts and personality traits. Astrology is based on the concept that everything is connected, and that our physical, mental, emotional and spiritual needs are affected by the planets. It is based on the principle "as above, so below".

Full astrological charts provide a map of potential. They show who a person can become, and reveal common themes we have already touched on in this book – strengths, weaknesses, gifts and challenges.

Even at our most basic level of knowledge, nearly everyone will know which star sign they are. For example, I'm a Leo. They are said to be courageous born leaders, here to express themselves creatively in the world. Leos are generous and give freely of their time. I can definitely apply those astrological insights to my life, and my purpose!

What about you? Have you stopped to consider the link between your star sign and who you are? Here's a very simple run down of the signs of the zodiac in terms of their focus, traits, and challenges.

Fire Signs – Aries, Leo, Sagittarius
Focus: To see what needs to be done, and do it.
Traits: Spontaneous, energetic, inspired, enthusiastic, visionary, intuitive, outgoing, passionate, playful
Challenges: Patience, pride, drama

Earth Signs – Capricorn, Taurus, Virgo,
Focus: To bring form to ideas and create tangible results.
Traits: Practical, resourceful, creative, supportive, productive, stable, grounded, dependable
Challenges: Flexibility, structure, service

Air Signs – Aquarius, Gemini, Libra
Focus: To bring clarity and new ideas.
Traits: Logical, analytical, objective, curious, thinkers, planners, intellectual, social, quick-witted
Challenges: Attention to detail, sensitivity, detachment

Water Signs – Pisces, Cancer, Scorpio
Focus: To bring out the best in others, nurture and heal.
Traits: Intuitive, emotional, sensitive, compassionate, adaptable, imaginative, nurturing, empathetic
Challenges: Logic, practicality, security, stability

As the saying goes, "it's written in the stars". I believe astrology is one of the tools that can help us understand who we really are, what we are here to learn, the gifts we need to harness, and our purpose in life. It can give us insights to our relationships, home and family, career, and personality.

The fuller art and science of astrology goes into detail about the alignment of the planets, zodiac and houses at the time of your birth and the influence these patterns of energy have on your life. If it interests you, delve into it further, and perhaps get an astrological chart drawn up. Or do your own research looking deeper for clues.

Numerology

Numerology is another tool you can use to understand at a deeper level who you are and what your purpose is. Much like astrology, numerology can reveal our gifts and talents, challenges and potential for this life. Numerology is the science of numbers used by the ancient Greeks and Egyptians.

The Greek philosopher, astronomer and astrologer, Pythagoras is generally accepted as the founder of modern day numerology. He said, "No one is free who has not obtained the empire of himself." In other words, to truly be you, you must understand, accept and embrace the totality of you.

Just like astrology, numerology doesn't make things happen, but it shows you your own potential. It's a powerful tool for more deeply understanding yourself.

Everything has a vibration, especially numbers. Numerology is based on the concept of order, where everything is perfectly balanced and harmonised, including the date of your birth and your birth name. Through numerology you can explore your birth day, life path, Soul personality, outer personality, destiny, karma, personal year cycles and much more.

Years ago I bought several books on numerology and spent months poring over the contents and having my own insights. At the time, if I'm honest, much of what I discovered sounded exciting but I really had no idea how to bring the potential into reality. Today when I look back on those notes, it's clear to me that my numerology held some remarkable insights into my path and purpose. Perhaps it was that exploration back then that fully unlocked my inner potential?

Let me share a couple of those insights.

My birth day number (as in the day I was born) is the 29th of the month. In numerology practice you add the two and the nine together, so it looks like this: 2+9=11. So 11 is my birth day number, which is also what's called a master number. The notes I wrote in my journal at the time said, "You are pure light, drawing people towards you to be inspired and uplifted. You must share your truth as a messenger of the world. Spiritual living is natural and you must follow your intuition." At the time I wrote that I recall thinking how amazing it sounded, and in truth it resonated for me but I had no idea how to embody it. Fast forward a few years and here I am. That reads like it's me to a tee.

My life path number is 4, or according to writer and spiritualist Dan Millman's model, 40:4. It means balancing inner gifts with structure and routine. Fours are good planners, and complete jobs thoroughly. Again, that's me to a tee. Despite my spiritual gifts, I often feel like I'm one of the most practical, logical people I know!

Another key aspect of who we are is our name. Every letter of the alphabet has a number vibration, and therefore every word has a vibration that perfectly describes its qualities. Take the word "love" for example. The values of the letters in the word (3+6+4+5=18; 1+8=9) add up to nine, which is the number that symbolises humanitarian unconditional love.

In numerology terms, my full birth name reveals my Soul or inner personality, my outer personality (or how the world sees me), and my destiny. (If you want to do this for yourself, get a numerology book to understand the process.) Looking back on my journal notes from all those years ago is interesting reading now. About my inner personality I wrote, "Ambitious hard worker. Life expects more of us than the average person, but we charge ahead regardless with strong inner stamina and an ability to overcome difficulties." Me? Yes, indeed. About my outer personality I wrote, "People who spread joy and good vibes, like the sun they light up the lives of everyone they meet. Others naturally gravitate towards them to feel happy and uplifted. Creative communicators." Again, all these years later that proves to be uncannily accurate. And as for my destiny number, which is master number 11, exactly the same as my birth number, essentially reaffirming that I am here to reconnect people to their own truth and inner spirit. Which I do through my work, my books and my programmes.

What about you? Does that all sound intriguing? Are you wondering what your numerology may reveal?

Here's a very simple run down of how to determine what your birth day number says about you. This is your most important number, according to numerology expert Suzanne Boult.

First determine your birth day number from the day on which you were born. For example, if you were born on the 7th of the month, your number is 7. If you were born on the 18th of the month add 1+8 together to get 9 as your number. The numbers 11 and 22 are master numbers and left as they are.

Then, see what that number says about your focus, gifts and challenges.

Number 1
Focus: To pioneer new and unique ways of doing things.
Gifts: Creative thinkers. Problem solvers. Practical. Organised.
Challenges: Strong-willed. Worrisome. Egotistical.

Number 2
Focus: To support others through peaceful collaboration.
Gifts: Flexible. Mediators. Intuitive. Caring.
Challenges: Indecisive. Reactive. Perfectionist.

Number 3
Focus: To inspire others and spread joy.
Gifts: Imaginative. Sociable. Clairvoyant. Artistic.
Challenges: Critical. Dramatic. Easily distracted.

Number 4
Focus: To use practicality and process to build solid foundations.
Gifts: Trust-worthy. Dependable. Unconventional. Methodical.
Challenges: Resistance. High expectations. Pessimistic.

Number 5
Focus: To be free to experience the fullness of life.
Gifts: Adaptable. Flexible. Fun-loving. Bright.
Challenges: Impulsive. Addictive personality. Easily bored.

Number 6
Focus: To serve lovingly and share beauty.
Gifts: Family-oriented. Nurturers. Generous. Healers.
Challenges: Responsibility. Discernment. Opinionated.

Number 7
Focus: To balance mental and emotional energy for inner peace.
Gifts: Psychic. Loyal. Knowledgeable. Thinkers.
Challenges: Discriminating. Easily disappointed. Restless.

Number 8
Focus: To balance power and success with happiness.
Gifts: Stamina. Ambition. Resourceful. Self-starters.
Challenges: Dominating. Intense. Misunderstood.

Number 9
Focus: To work from the heart for humanity.
Gifts: Compassionate. Gentle. Forgiving. Courageous.
Challenges: Impatient. High ideals. Letting go.

Master Number 11
Focus: To be a messenger who uplifts and inspires.
Gifts: Visionary. Spiritual. Teacher. Dreamer.
Challenges: Obsessive. Prioritising. Trust.

Master Number 22
Focus: To build new foundations for humanity.
Gifts: Manifestation. Spiritual. Ingenious. Builder.
Challenges: Overwhelm. Fear of failure. Nervousness.

With both astrology and numerology, be aware of any recurring themes, like my double number 11. Something that comes up two or three times, or more, is probably a major theme of your purpose.

Exploring numerology can be so insightful! Personally, I love it. And if it has intrigued you in any way, I do encourage you to investigate further for yourself.

The point is this: your Soul has ensured there is a not-so-hidden trail and if you choose to follow it, you will be surprised at just how much you discover your own truth. We'd need a whole book to explore numerology thoroughly, so I encourage you to go and research your own numerological patterns and to understand the insights they can provide you. You may be surprised!

Signs and synchronicities

We are constantly receiving information and guidance to help us on our path, and this is just another way the Universe affirms for us what we already know. It is giving us another piece of our 'purpose puzzle'.

As if to remind us of who we really are and to keep us most aligned to our original intention for being here, we have experiences like déjà vu, synchronicities and signs.

We've all had those moments. Something, usually unexpected, happens and we think to ourselves, *Wow, what are the odds of that happening?* There are those moments when you look back on the events or experiences leading up to something significant, connecting the dots as I like to say. Or those moments when you seem to see the same things happening repeatedly in your world, leading you in a certain direction or affirming the choices you have made. If you have had similar experiences then you have undoubtedly experienced signs and synchronicities at work.

Synchronicities and signs could be considered meaningful coincidences. But, to me, really they aren't coincidental at all. A blind date that leads to happily ever after. A lottery win when the bank is foreclosing on a mortgage. A dream that turns out to be true. An opportunity for the job we never thought we'd get. A faulty traffic light signal that pulls you back from possible tragedy. There are no coincidences. There may be experiences or circumstances that are unplanned or unexpected. But they are not coincidence.

Sometimes signs or synchronicities are so huge it's hard to ignore them. Other times, they can go unnoticed, especially if you tend to hurry through life without time to pause and reflect on your days. So in reality, these happenings can occur on a large, medium or small scale.

Large ones are just that. They have a major impact. Like meeting your Soul love, experiencing a significant personal tragedy, or being made redundant from your job. The medium ones are more like course correcting moments.

They lead us on to the bigger synchronicities. For example you may have a run of medium-level experiences leading you to a major moment, like, you get an unexpected pay rise, which allows you to take your first holiday in years during which you find your future husband (that's a major one). You get the idea.

We are always trying to move forward in life and synchronicities are the Universe's way of rejigging things to help us. The small events and signs are equally important, as they are like fine-tuning each step.

I like to think of synchronicities as little miracles. Usually they are confirmation of where you are at in that moment. This is why attention to the daily detail in your life is so important. You could easily miss a series of little fine-tuning synchronicities. Pay special attention to anything that happens three or more times. Look for patterns and repeated themes, and often these could be symbolic and in need of some deeper pondering.

And remember, when you are living in vibration with who you really are, life flows. Things fall into place, as if by magic. The flow is interrupted, and we encounter blocks when we become off path.

If you stopped to think of say the last 20 years of your life, and started 'connecting the dots', what might be some of the major signs, events or synchronicities that have all added up to where you are right now?

To help you, here's a glimpse of some of the major connecting the dots moments in my life (this timeline was sprinkled with untold medium and small signs, events and synchronicities too):

- Lose everything but my life in a house fire (2003)
- Shed 20kgs in weight (2004)
- Marry and then separate from my first husband (2005)
- Meet my Soul love (2005)
- Marry my Soul love (2009)
- Receive my first Reiki attunement that leads to a spiritual awakening (2009)

I spent the next two years simultaneously trying to listen to and ignore my inner spirit, which was calling me to make radical life changes that would realign me to my Purpose. The major events continued to flow:

- Sell property and downsize our life (2010)
- Resign from my job and my career (2011)
- Start my own business (2011)
- Publish my first book (2012)
- Win three international book awards (2013)

Even just doing this small exercise, it is interesting to see how quickly my life has changed and accelerated with major events the more on path I became. No doubt you will notice patterns in your own life too.

So, contrary to what you may think, who you are and your purpose in life is not a great mystery. There is no initiation to go through. No arduous task to undertake. No spiritual pilgrimage required. The answers to all your greatest questions about life are closer than you think. You already know far more about yourself and your purpose than you have probably ever realised. You simply need to pause and remember. Follow the trail. Because it's not so secret after all.

Simple reflection

It is important that you take the time now to reassemble the contents of your toolkit for this life and your Soul purpose. This simple reflection will guide you to look with fresh eyes at your childhood and consider the signs and synchronicities in your life so far. As always, use your journal or turn to the relevant page in the Soul Happiness companion workbook.

Childhood memories

Reflect on your family life. Allow your mind to drift back to your earliest childhood memories. Gradually bring yourself up through the years until your late teens. In your journal record your answers to these questions.

- What was your family dynamic like when you were growing up?
- How many siblings do you have, where do you fall in the birth order?
- What traits or qualities have you learned from your parents and your grandparents?
- Were there beliefs that infused your family?
- What did you most enjoy doing with your time?
- What games did you like to play?
- What were your favourite subjects in school as a child?
- What were you really good at?
- Did you have a favourite toy or book?
- Where were your favourite places to go?
- What insights do the answers to these questions bring?

Connecting your dots

We all have significant moments or events that perhaps at the time don't seem so significant, but in hindsight created a new opportunity or started a chain of events in our life. It's useful to see how synchronicities have already been at work in your own life.

- Draw a vertical line down a fresh page in your journal to represent the timeline of your life.
- Decide a period of time, say the last 10 or 20 years of your life, in which you will recall significant events or synchronicities that had a major impact on your life or the direction it took.
- At the top of the line, put a mark and write the first event and the date it happened.
- Work down the line noting more significant events, signs or synchronicities until you reach current time.
- Then ponder. What does this timeline reveal to you? What have you learnt about yourself through this exercise?

Simple promise

Make this simple promise to yourself now. Remind yourself of this promise throughout your day or write it down where you will see it.

I see my life with loving eyes and create the space for my Soul to expand.

Simple practices

These simple steps can help you put the ideas in this chapter into practice. Remember, there is power in doing something. Anything. Just one thing. Because the moment you do, you make a conscious change in your life.

Ask questions. If you have trouble with childhood memories, talk to your siblings, parents or grandparents. What do they remember about you? What do they recall you like to do, or play at? What childhood traits most stand out for them?

Be gentle. Be gentle on yourself. The answers are within you, you simply need to create the space and the awareness for the information to return to you.

Consult an expert. Investigate astrology or numerology. Look further into what they may say about your inner self and your purpose. Consult an expert and get professional readings.

Create a memory bank. Gather photos, and any childhood icons you may have – favourite toys, gifts, treasured books. Allow these items to trigger memories. Take a week and spend time each day writing stories and memories from your childhood.

Notice signs. Become aware of signs and synchronicities in your life as they happen. Record them as they happen and see if there is a pattern, for example repetitive numbers. Look deeper. What does this tell you?

Read. If you feel there is more in your childhood memories than you know how to access, consider reading specialist books on unlocking the secrets of childhood memories, or seek some professional assistance.

PART TWO

be in soul flow

Life calls us to dream and when we take action, our dreams

come to life in ways we might never have imagined.

The first part of this book showed you a deeper connection with yourself and your Soul's purpose. It was about helping you align with the truth of who you are and your limitless potential.

Now, in this part, you will learn how to harness that Soul connection and start bringing your inner and outer worlds into alignment. That is Soul flow. The chapters that follow give you the secrets to anchoring your purpose in your life, and living authentically to create the space for Soul growth. It will show you that when you integrate the spiritual and the physical, in an ordered way, you have the power to manifest whatever it is you want for yourself.

The more you see and live your own truth – not anyone else's – the more deep happiness you will experience in your life. Allowing yourself to be who you are, loving yourself unconditionally no matter what, and honouring the pull to follow your bliss is what Soul happiness is all about.

CHAPTER 7

secret 7: say yes to your soul

Every moment lived adds another stitch, and even if you cannot envision what the final pattern will look like, it helps to know the thread is golden.
~ Deepak Chopra

The secret of Soul purpose, and therefore Soul happiness, is simple. It's the inner before the outer. As with everything in life, the most important relationship we will ever have is with ourselves. Knowing ourselves, connecting to our true Soul-self, is our key mission. From there, everything about our outer life will flow.

To feel like you have purpose in life there's only one thing you need to do: say yes to your Soul-self. It knows what you really want, what you desire, what you love. It knows your gifts and strengths and passions. When you say yes to your Soul-self, you automatically align with your path and purpose. Because you are the path.

And you know what happened for me when I started honouring my Soul-self? After getting over the scary, at times illogical, even downright crazy decisions it wanted me to make – like quitting my high-flying career, and selling beautiful homes and gorgeous possessions to downsize our life? I got into Soul flow.

I had to overcome my biggest inner demons first. The fear of being judged. The fear of not being good enough. The fear of letting go of my 'identity' – who would I be without my big job and my big life? The fear of failing. The fear of trusting myself. The fear of putting myself first. The fear of indulging my passions.

I had to shed my illusions and false truths. *I'm only lovable if I'm successful. I need to be successful for myself, and others, to be proud of me. Who I am is what I have. I have to struggle in life to get anywhere.*

All of this, and more, allowed me to finally see my truth. My life according to the real me. Not my life according to my perceived expectations of my parents. Or my boss. Or my employees. Or my husband. Or my friends.

My life. Deeper than that. Me.

I've realised that's what inner purpose is all about. Seeing your truth. Understanding your Soul's code. Saying yes to your Soul-self. Making choices that honour you.

When you do that, life can't help but re-order itself to fit your new brief. Every moment you step closer to who you are within, is a call for your outer path to respond. Your outer purpose will rise to meet your inner awakening.

What you think your purpose is, and where you actually end up can be quite different, as I discovered.

Stepping onto my new path of self-employment, I wanted everything to fit neatly into a box. I thought, *I'll just have my own business, work individually with people, have enough to live on. That's all I need.*

It was clear my Soul-self had other plans and that I had set out on a significant alignment with my purpose.

Within three months my first book idea was born, and in a state of beautiful Soul flow, I wrote *Beyond Happiness* in just eight weeks. The flow continued. My business doubled, and then tripled. My waiting list grew from one month, to two, to three, to four. What I thought would be just one book, turned into a series. At a moment of self-doubt, when I was deeply questioning *Who am I to think I can be an author of anything people wish to read?* I received one of my biggest signs so far. A triple award win for *Beyond Happiness*, with it being named the best book of the year in its class. I love how the Universe works. I could have dismissed one award as a fluke. Two

Soul Happiness

as coincidence. But three? Well you can't really argue with that.

The more my inner and outer worlds align, the more I am truly *me* in all parts of my life, the more I really get into Soul flow. TV appearances, speaking gigs, the money I need at exactly the right time. Books running off shelves the moment they get in-store. That's how I know I am in tune with my purpose – inner and outer.

It's clear that my view of where this path is going compared to the expansiveness of my potential are worlds apart. All I can do is keep trusting myself, honouring my guidance, following my heart, and having faith that each next step will be revealed to me at the perfect time.

And that is all you can do too. Honour yourself first. Then do what you love. Those are two simple keys to Soul happiness.

The secret of purpose

Knowing ourselves, connecting to our true Soul-self, is our key mission. From there, everything about our outer life will flow. It's really that simple: inner before outer.

Becoming the most radiant, enlightened you is why you are here. Awakening to your true power is why you are here. Expressing the true you, your Soul-self, is *why you are here.*

Your inner purpose provides the foundation and structure for your outer purpose and, ultimately, Soul happiness. Your inner purpose creates the space, the courage, the passion, the focus, the belief and the energy you need to embrace your outer purpose. It is the 'being' part of your purpose.

As I wrote in *Beyond Happiness*:

> *When you connect to your true self, everything becomes clear. Sometimes it is a slow dawning; other times it is an instant recognition. However it happens for you, you will be forever changed. You will see your life through*

105

new eyes. You will see that everything is beautiful, everything is a wonder, and everything is true. It's as if you can look at yourself for the first time and actually see you, not just the projection of you. Your true purpose in life lies not in an outward expression of brilliance but in seeing the shining brilliance of your true self. When you connect with your true self, you open up the lines of communication to tap into your Soul purpose and see your true potential in this life.

Choosing to be authentically you in your life is the only way to tap into inner happiness and joy. Only then can you truly express your outer purpose.

Your inner purpose is the true inner you. Your Soul-self. Honouring who you truly are is your inner purpose, and then living a life in tune with who you are is your outer purpose. You are connected to these inner aspects of your being through your feelings.

Although it may seem confusing, purpose is actually very simple. Just decide how you want to be, and then be it. Align your inner and your outer and the rest of your purpose will flow. Focus simply on who you are being in each aspect of your life. By doing so, you will automatically move closer to your true self. With every step you are simply polishing, refining, revealing what has always been there. Who you really are. You are stepping into your full Soul power.

Purpose automatically conjures feelings of having to 'do something'. The reality is that it's far more simple than that.

Most of us tend to focus on the outer aspect of our lives. What we're here to do, what we have, the identities we have. But purpose isn't necessarily a job, or a set of responsibilities, or even a list of goals. It doesn't have a label, and it cannot be boxed.

Purpose is not a 'thing'. Like your Soul, purpose is fluid, changeable, adaptable. It just is. It is more about a calling. A deep urge to express yourself and be a certain way.

Even with all the reflection, dot-connecting, and a-ha moments you may have had so far in this book, it's possible you still don't feel crystal clear about your purpose. And that's ok. It's ok if you can't just squeeze all the goodness out on cue. It's ok if you can't think of anything that seems especially meaningful to you. All it means is that you need to give yourself more time.

Know that purpose grows as we do. And when you create the space for it, purpose will reveal itself. As you say yes to yourself, so does purpose. As you trust, so does purpose. It is a co-operative; the more you give, the more your Soul gives. You and your Soul are working together and the more you wish to grow, the more you will.

Purpose is so intertwined with who we are, that when we have meaning and purpose, when we act with love, and when we honour ourselves, we have Soul happiness. Happiness is based on a life of meaning, where our existence doesn't compromise our Soul's code.

Your Soul map

The purpose of this book is to help you start creating the space for answers to your deepest questions about your life.

When it comes to your purpose, all you need is clarity. With clarity comes intention, and when action follows intention that's all you need to align your inner and outer worlds.

We can go our whole lives without really knowing who we truly are. Creating your own Soul map will ensure you understand your deepest desires and your true self like never before. It's like coming home. Because that's what it is. So when you get there, it feels familiar, exciting, freeing, beautiful. You feel like even though it may scare you, that this is really and truly *you*.

Creating your Soul map

Your Soul map is the blueprint for your purpose. It's one of the most beneficial practices you can have to get clear on why you're here. When you blend it with your life planning, it will help you align your inner and outer worlds and say yes to yourself with ease.

The four aspects of your Soul code combine to help you determine your Soul map. You will have gathered more information than you realise with the Soul code reflection exercises in the previous chapters.

Let's briefly recap the Soul's code, and how everything fits together.

There are four aspects of your Soul code linking and intertwining across your inner and outer purpose.

Your challenges and values give you key insights to your inner purpose.
- Your Soul challenges show you what you need to learn and embody.
- You Soul values show you your deepest desires and guiding principles for life.

Your gifts, passions and Soul path give you insights to your outer purpose.
- Your Soul character shows you your innate gifts and passions to share.
- Your Soul path gives you deeper insight to the purpose you were born with, and allows you to connect the dots in your life.

Essentially you are taking your insights from the previous chapters, and distilling them into a succinct map. The Soul map looks like this:

SOUL MAP

GUIDING PRINCIPLES	OUTER PURPOSE
WHAT'S IMPORTANT TO YOU?	HOW AM I TO SERVE OTHERS?
Your innermost values. The things you most love, appreciate or wish to embody in your life. One for each key life area: Purpose + Spirit, Lifestyle + Living, Love + Relationships, Health + Wellbeing	*The value you will create in the world. Your outer purpose. Expressed as a single "I am" statement.*
INNER FOCUS	**SOUL CHARACTER**
HOW AM I TO SERVE MYSELF?	WHO YOU WANT TO BE + HOW DO YOU WANT TO FEEL?
What you need to welcome into your life. The inner belief or lesson you need to embrace, your inner purpose. Expressed as a single "I am" statement.	*The innate qualities, strengths and passions you want to embody and share. Aim for 6-8 across the inner and outer aspects of your life.*

Refer to the guidelines at the end of this chapter for the steps to complete your Soul map. And if you need more help, try this process.

- **Set your intention.** Any practice undertaken with the conscious intention that it will reveal more about your Soul path will lead to you receiving more information. It will work. Answers might not appear instantly (then again, they might). Keep focused. Be open. And let go of your limiting beliefs.

- **Ask.** Choose your questions carefully. Use some of the questions that appear throughout this book. Ask yourself, *What do I love? How can I do it? Who can I help? What value can I create? How am I to serve myself? How am I to serve others?* Write down what you feel and stay focused so as to not wander off course. Ask follow up questions if needed. Writing it down is so important. I've always done this for myself, and love reading over them in the months and years that follow. There are always revealing patterns or insights that I didn't see the first time – like some of my numerology insights I shared in the previous chapter. Keeping track and keeping a record gives you the opportunity to make sense of things in the future when you may have a different perspective. Plus, writing things down allows your guidance to flow, as your mind is distracted with the act of writing.

- **Be patient.** Patience is a toughie. Especially if you're like me and you want all the answers right now. The truth is, sometimes we're not ready for the answers and we have to wait until we are before they will come. Forcing it is not going to get you anywhere. If you feel like answers aren't forthcoming for you, just leave it for a while. Days or weeks if you have to. I guarantee that you will get some real clarity when you least expect it. Like when you're hanging out washing, or doing your hair, or chopping vegetables for dinner. Sometimes we just need to give our mind a break, to let our true guidance come to awareness.

- **Connect the dots.** If you look carefully, you might already be able to see a pattern forming. The things that light you up, that other people always compliment you on, the activities that you really enjoy, those are all dots pointing the way to your purpose. You were put on this marvellous Earth to do what you love. No exceptions.

- **Trust your guidance.** I read once that if you asked the question, *What is the true purpose of my Soul?*, and wrote the answer over, and over, and over again, until you wrote the answer that made you cry, that was how you knew it was your Soul truth. You could do that. But more importantly, when you start a process like this you need to trust yourself. You're starting now, because the time is perfect right now. Because you're ready. Because your inner guidance has gems of brilliance it has been waiting to share with you. Don't dismiss yourself with thoughts like *I'm just making that up. That doesn't make sense.*

That's not what I thought it would be. When you ask for guidance, you will get it, and you must trust it.

- **Follow your bliss.** An important part of your Soul purpose and Soul happiness is to follow your bliss. Once you know what you love, what you're deeply passionate about, do it. So many people don't. So choose to be someone who gives themselves permission to do more of what they love. If you know it, you must do it! Trust it, follow it, even if you think it's not taking you where you think it ought to. Chances are it's where you need to go, and you'll end up someplace better. When you follow your bliss, you naturally get on the right path. Doors open. Money appears. Opportunities tap you on the shoulder. Because the Universe always supports us when we are on path and on purpose.

Using your Soul map

Here's where most of us get it wrong. We think we have to find our purpose. Remember, your purpose already *is*. Your purpose will find you. You simply have to create the space for it to show up and make itself known. And your Soul map is the perfect space.

So you've completed your Soul map. Now what? What do you *do* with it?

Well, think of your Soul map as a blueprint, an anchor, a compass for your life. It's a vitally important guiding tool in your life. It very clearly spells out what's important to you.

At times when you find yourself turning big questions over and over in your mind, or when faced with a major life decision, your Soul map will give you the answer. It's your own sacred Soul oracle quietly reminding you of your inner truth.

Do you want to do extended travel overseas? What does your Soul map say? If you have freedom, adventure and excitement as part of your Soul map, it's likely this choice will be the right one. A feast for your senses and your spirit. But if your Soul map is more about safety and security and planning, it may be that this choice isn't in alignment with all you value.

Do you want to go for that high-powered corporate promotion? What does your Soul map say? If you've identified engagement, energy and innovation as part of your Soul map, then dive in headfirst. Feel your heart soar as you take the next step. But if your Soul map is filled with words like community, service and creativity, perhaps you'd be better aligned by sharing your gifts in another way.

Use your Soul map to guide you in life. To determine which path most reflects your highest truth. To align your choices with your values. Using it will help you stay in Soul flow and as close to your Soul path as possible.

Your Soul map isn't fixed. It isn't something you can 'set and forget'. Your Soul map is not a static document. It is organic, dynamic, it will change over time. Just as you grow and evolve, so too should it grow with you. In fact, the more you grow, and the more open you are to reaching your full inner and outer potential, the more it will reflect the possibility of all that you are back to you.

And so my guidance is to review your Soul map frequently, rather than file it away. You may like to make the reflection on your Soul map an annual ritual in your life. Or perhaps monthly, perhaps every six months, perhaps every new moon – whatever works for you. Re-read it, re-feel it. How is it resonating with you? What's feeling really good? Where are you off track? Where are you oh-so-close, and what can you tweak to make sure that you align even further with your truth?

Your Soul map only has as much power as you give it. You need to actively continue to use it and update it and infuse it with your essence.

When you do that, it will act as a life-changing tool. It's seriously magical stuff.

Understanding your Soul map

You Soul map will have meaning for you. And it will give you the insights, confidence and trust to live a life in tune with who you really are.

Let me tell you about Paula. She is a 40 year old mother of two, who works part time in a hair salon. Before she got married she was a well-known artist in amateur circles. She had received a few commissions, held exhibitions and made a reasonable living from her art. Creative expression is when she truly feels connected and yet she gave it away when she became a wife and mother. She retrained as a hairdresser, something she could fit into her schedule and earn a regular income from. Although creative in a sense, it was the 'real' job she felt she needed to get which could help provide for her family.

Two years ago she started having panic attacks and feeling desperately unhappy. Her doctor said she was depressed and prescribed anti-depressants. She felt there had to be something more to life and she started meditation and yoga as a way of helping her stay grounded and peaceful. Unexpectedly she started to think a lot about her early years as an artist. To the point where she unboxed some of her old work and supplies.

Paula started reflecting on her own life path, values, passions and more. She knew she had gone way off path in her life, stepping away from the joy she received through her art. She started contemplating her purpose. She realised an aspect of her hairdressing role she most enjoyed was training and mentoring her younger colleagues. Paula started making many changes in her life, committing to being creative through her art and making time for herself every day. She found greater inner peace and clarity and no longer needed to take medication to help her keep centred. She was asked to display some of her art in a local gallery, and was approached by someone intrigued by her unique style and wanting private tuition. Before long, Paula recognised a business opportunity, providing creative workshops and wellbeing events. She loved helping people express their inner creativity. Within a year Paula had franchised her business.

Paula's completed Soul map is below. She knows how valuable it would have been to have a blueprint to guide her years ago.

PAULA'S SOUL MAP

GUIDING PRINCIPLES	**OUTER PURPOSE**
Purpose + Spirit:	*I am a creative teacher,*
To unconditionally love myself	*bringing joy to others and*
and others.	*inspiring them to see their full*
Lifestyle + Living:	*potential.*
To allow continued growth and	
expression in my life.	
Love + Relationships:	
To be giving and generous of spirit.	
Health + Wellbeing:	
To balance and harmonise every	
part of my life.	
INNER FOCUS	**SOUL CHARACTER**
I am free to combine my passions	***Inner:*** *Inspired. Mindful.*
and be creative and prosperous.	*Energised. Nourished.*
	Outer: *Colourful. Determined.*
	Grateful. Expansive.

And let me share Melissa's story with you too. Melissa completed her Soul map and found it invaluable for navigating some delicate and daunting decisions in her life.

Melissa is in her late twenties. She went to law school and ended up working in a well-paid job in the government. After several promotions in as many years she was feeling more and more despondent. She knew in her bones that what she was doing just wasn't right for her. The problem was she had no idea what *was* right for her. She didn't know what she should be doing with her life. She felt lost and confused.

Melissa started working through the Soul map process. With every step Melissa only felt more and more affirmation that her constricting legislative job and her money-oriented lifestyle zapped her energy more than it fed her spirit. It might have been perfect for her colleagues, but it was far from perfect for her.

She knew it would make absolutely no sense to anyone else, but she'd been secretly daydreaming about resigning and selling everything to move to the beach and set up an online business. She loved quirky homewares and furnishings and knew there was a real niche to be had. And her frequent 12-hour days meant there was no time in Melissa's life for the things she loved to do.

The sensible Melissa kept quashing the idea. Yet the risk-taker in her already had research, contacts, suppliers and more filed away after more than a year of flirting with the idea.

At a point in her life where Melissa felt at a complete crossroads, her completed Soul map gave her a clear and decisive steer in the direction that was most aligned to her purpose.

Now, three years after she threw caution to the wind, bundled up all her belongings and chose a simpler life for herself, Melissa does own and run that online business. It quickly grew to a six-figure annual turnover with a worldwide supplier and logistics network that she runs from her beautiful home office overlooking the sea. And the best bit? Melissa works on average a couple of hours a day, leaving plenty of time for her other passions: surfing, hiking, and spending time with her new love Sam and their dogs Ringo and Star.

This is Melissa's Soul map. She says she feels like she's living the dream, and she knows she wouldn't have had the faith to change her life without her Soul map.

MELISSA'S SOUL MAP

GUIDING PRINCIPLES	**OUTER PURPOSE**
Purpose + Spirit:	*I am a connector, bringing people*
To live freely and to have choice.	*and opportunities together*
Lifestyle + Living:	*to create beautiful lives.*
To see new ways of doing things, to	
express myself creatively.	
Love + Relationships:	
To make a positive difference.	
Health + Wellbeing:	
To feel inner-calm and serenity.	
INNER FOCUS	**SOUL CHARACTER**
I am limitless when I honour	***Inner:*** *Spirited. Balanced.*
the truth in my heart.	*Curious. Excited.*
	Outer: *Vibrant. Free.*
	Expressive. Beauty.

Rest assured, I'm not trying to play down the intricacies of purpose. Or make out that it's easy to realise your dreams. Or imply that life changes are made with seamless transitions. But if you want to do something, you can. And you'll know it's right because of how you feel. Your Soul map is your check-in tool for life.

Purpose is what's true for you

For most of us the reality is that we have chosen something great to do, or be, or give while we are here. And on some level – be it conscious or Soul – you already know what it is.

So, right now it's time to make a very important mental 'note to self'. Everyone is on a different Soul journey. That includes you. Some people are here to do world changing stuff; some people are here to change the world for just a few. Both paths are perfect.

Soul purpose is not necessarily huge or grand. That's where most of us get it wrong. We make ourselves feel less than ok if we are completely, utterly perfect just being who we are and doing what we're doing.

Just like in school, some Souls will be in their final years and others will just be beginning. You cannot compare your journey to anyone else's. What is true for you, what feels right for you, is perfect. Some people may have an entire purpose focused on feeling safe and secure in life. Or allowing themselves to become independent and recognised in their field. Or in parenting a gorgeous Soul with an important future purpose. There is no difference between a lofty purpose to cure cancer and a purpose some may view as everyday, like making toys for kids.

To illustrate this further, I'm reminded of a television programme I like watching called 'The Secret Millionaire'. It's where wealthy people go undercover in a needy community, meet the people, understand their stories, and connect with who they really are. The idea is then that the millionaire decides how much of their own money to give to different people, families or causes and their true identity is revealed when they present the cheque.

I watched an episode where someone refused to take the money offered to them, an amount of about £15,000. The millionaire was so moved by this man who worked at the local council dump, where he would rescue broken and unwanted bikes and toys and, out of his own money, he would return them to working order. He did this so that underprivileged children in his neighbourhood got to own a bike, or have presents at Christmas. This man lived a very simple life; he was content to have milk in the fridge, bread in the cupboard, pay his bills, and to give the rest of his money away for the simple joy of making other people happy. He even returned lost wallets to their owners, putting his own money into their wallets for good luck. He'd spent £3,000 of his own money alone doing that. The millionaire wanted to support the good work this man was doing in his community and was thoroughly surprised when he declined the generous gift. He simply said he was doing what he knew he was meant to be doing. He didn't need a lot for himself and his greatest joy came from the joy of others. A simple man at heart, a simple man in life, yet a man completely sure of his own purpose.

Before we go any further, keep yourself in check with how you are feeling as you work your way through the rest of this book. Your purpose could be the most simple, everyday thing, or it could be the most wide-reaching, world-changing thing. It doesn't matter. There is no competition around purpose. Just remember, your purpose is whatever fills your heart with love. It's what is true for you and no Soul ever denies itself when it is on purpose.

While it's important not to judge the size or scale of your purpose, also remember not to play too small either. It saddens me that so many of us seem conditioned to believe that we are no one. We think we're not special or talented. How can we possibly do anything life-changing for others, let alone world changing?

Just remember, the most influential, ground breaking, inspirational, life-changing, world-changing people throughout history started out just like you. Until you learn to master it, your conscious mind – or your ego – likes you to believe that you're not as beautiful, talented and amazing as you really are. It delights in illusion, hiding you from your true power and trapping you in the vicious cycles of what you think you have to accept as your life, and what you think you need to be happy.

It's this part of ourselves that sets endless limitations. How much money we can earn and how long it will take. How much love we are allowed. How happy we can feel. How much goodness we are entitled to in our lives.

Even when you start exploring your purpose, it's likely that part of you will put a limit on just how bold or big or beautiful it will be. Those limits are based on your views of yourself and your life. They are based on safety and security and the bounds of our 'comfort zone'.

And, it's ok. Sometimes it's big enough and scary enough just to take the first steps towards purpose. And honestly, I believe so many of us would shrink in self-doubt and fear if we truly understood how amazing we really are and what we are here to do.

So, start small. Just start.

Think about it like this. If acting is your deep passion, but all you've ever done is local theatre productions, you have two choices. You can decide that local theatre is just enough for you. And that's ok. But if you feel a Soul urge to indulge that passion and talent further, if you dream of being an A-list star, you might start by auditioning for television advertisements. But you know you have more to offer, so you secure an agent and invest in yourself with acting lessons. When the time is right you start attending auditions for television roles, and you know it's the right thing to do. But to be true to your values you turn down a part that you feel objectifies women. You fear that decision could be the end of your career but you persevere and you land a break-out role in a critically acclaimed show. You feel like you've really hit your stride and can fully express yourself as an actress. You feel like life is flowing and you land the perfect leading role in a movie with your dream director. You feel as though you have stepped into your full power. You become that A-list star. And you realise there is further work for you to do. You use your power, your face, your name, your following, for the good of others through charitable environmental and humanitarian work around the world. It is then that you feel like you have attained your true purpose, and you establish your own international organisation at the forefront of women's rights in third world countries. You author a book about your work and become an advisor to governments and agencies around the world. Your acting continues, but instead of being a vehicle for your stardom, you now see that it is a vehicle for you to do what you were always meant to. And you look back and marvel at your journey. You realise that if someone had told you way back at the start that this is where you would end up, you would've been too overwhelmed to ever allow yourself to move past local theatre.

The point of this story is this: have your dreams, but know they are usually limited by your own beliefs. In reality, something much more awesome lies beyond and the closer you get to it, the clearer it will become.

So, don't for a minute think that your life is your lot. Don't get caught up in believing that you're too old. Too young. Not smart enough. Not thin enough. Too poor. Time poor. Don't know where to start.

You are here for a reason. And when the time is right you will know exactly what that is. And when you choose to honour that, another step will become clear and you will reveal an even deeper aspect of your purpose. And then you will step again. And grow more, share more, shine more. It is inevitable. The choice is always yours.

So by giving yourself permission to follow your bliss, you naturally give yourself permission to follow your purpose. The link between bliss and purpose is intrinsic. So be and do more of what you love right now.

I often say we most resist what we most need. It may very well be that the thing you have shied away from, the thing that makes you feel different, the very thing you fear may make you stand out, is exactly what you need to honour. It may very well be the thing in your life that will have the most impact on others as well as yourself.

Again, the people we now recognise as making history, making discoveries, and making our world beautiful were the people who were thought of as different, eccentric, and even a little strange. When you follow your inner guidance and lead with your heart, you become one of those amazing, courageous people. Love yourself. Shine your light. You are special; embrace it. Stand taller, speak with conviction, and believe you are important.

✻

Simple reflection

This is the chapter where you get to pull all the insights from your Soul code together; it's the bridge between syncing with your Soul and being in Soul flow.

Your Soul map

Turn to a new page in your journal, or the relevant page in the Soul Happiness companion workbook.

- Draw four boxes on the page, one each for inner focus, Soul character, guiding principles and outer purpose.
- Complete your Soul map referring to the reflection exercise you have completed in the preceding chapters. Refer to the guidelines and examples on pages 109-116.
- Revisit your Soul map at least annually. Ask yourself: *What's changed? What's clearer now? What do I want to do more of? Less of?*
- Remember, your Soul map is your blueprint for your purpose. It's one of the most beneficial practices you can have to get clear on why you're here. When you blend it with your life planning, it will help you align your inner and outer worlds.

An alternative approach:

If you feel stuck trying to complete your Soul map, use this process:

- List everything you love and all the values, beliefs and gifts you can connect with. *(Soul character)*
- Then decide how you can do these things and what value you can create. *(Guiding principles)*
- Then list everything and everyone you believe you can help.
- Then write two statements that answer the following questions:

How am I to serve myself? (inner focus) How am I to serve others? (outer purpose)

Simple promise

Make this simple promise to yourself now. Remind yourself of this promise throughout your day or write it down where you will see it.

My purpose is what I know to be true for me.

Simple practices

These simple steps can help you put the ideas in this chapter into practice. Remember, there is power in doing something. Anything. Just one thing. Because the moment you do, you make a conscious change in your life.

Be methodical. An ordered, repetitive and consistent approach to anything in your life will create the environment for ideas, insight and inspiration to flow and get results. This is as true for a work project, as it is for reconnecting to yourself and your purpose.

Know what your heart wants. Remember, purpose is simply aligning to your deepest desires. For that, tune into the knowing of your heart.

Practice stillness. Do anything that brings moments of silence and stillness into your life. These are the moments when you have the most clarity.

Trust yourself. You already know far more than you realise. Start honouring the inner voice of your heart and trusting it will guide you true.

♡

simple meditation

Embrace Purpose

Get comfortable in your meditation space.

Breathe in through your nose and out through your mouth.

Breathe in love. Deeply.

Breathe out anger. Relax.

Breathe in joyful happiness.

Breathe out fear. Let go.

Breathe in your truth.

Breathe out limitation.

Feel the spread of inner awakening.

Become one with your true purpose.

Step into your life with knowing.

See your dreams unfold with ease.

Know all your desire is yours.

Soulfully. Blissfully. For life.

And so it is.

CHAPTER 8

secret 8: create your reality

Happiness is an expression of the Soul in considered actions.
~ Marcus Aurelius

A key aspect of being in Soul flow is to take soulful action in the direction of your dreams. When you take action you open your arms wide to receive more of everything you desire.

This chapter will guide you to bring your dreams to life by aligning your inner and outer worlds. It's about infusing your values, and your passions in your life, and aligning the dreams you have for your life with your purpose.

The reason we feel out of balance in parts of our life at any one time is because when we fail to make a conscious choice about how to live our lives, our conscious mind – our ego self – takes over. The conscious mind creates what it perceives you need – based on a whole lot of external patterns and internal beliefs. Without a focused plan, the conscious mind has free reign. It can create whatever it wants. Or whatever it thinks you want.

This is why we so often end up in repeating patterns or situations. We fail to realise we are in control of the reset button and we are in control of the plan.

So to be sure your mind is busy creating what you really want, you need to make sure it's got the plan that you want it to work to. If you want something different, choose to believe something different.

The importance of making plans is that you are programming your conscious mind with your new reality. You are setting the intention for how you want things to be.

Until I started setting intentions and having plans, the part of me that thinks it knows best used to charge off creating the life it thought I had to have.

My 20s were the prime example. I thought that in order to be happy, I needed someone to love me. So I would choose someone to fill that role. The wrong someone. Over and over again. I thought that to be successful I had to do everything myself, that asking for help was a weakness. So I worked my tail off. Overtime, again and again. I thought that to make people proud, I had to have titles and achieve things. So, I chose security over adventure. Job promotions and home ownership over feeding my senses with travel, culture, and inspiration.

And I blindly overlooked the mounting signs that I had it all very, very wrong. That I was out of sync with my Soul-self. The more this cycle played out, the more my Soul-self was saying *Stop. Listen. Love yourself more than this.* If only I'd paused long enough to see it.

I acted as though I was a passive participant in my own life. Not in charge. Not setting my own direction. And I got very, very off course. So far off course I needed a massive course correction. Mine was a house fire, as you've read. But worse than the house fire. Worse than waking up amidst smoke and flames. Worse than discovering the fire was deliberately lit by a forever faceless no-name. Was losing everything I believed defined me.

From that point on I had to make different choices. I had to take charge. I had to rebuild my life. Rebuild me. I had decisions to make.

But the biggest thing I learnt was that my beliefs, thoughts and feelings create my world. If I want to change something I have to see it differently and, more importantly, I have to act differently.

I've come such a long way since then. Now, I decide how I want to feel and then plan to do what I need to do to infuse that feeling into my life. And when I do this, straight-up magic happens.

I know that if I am clear about who I am, how I want to feel and therefore why I want what I want, life unfolds in accordance with how I truly want it to happen.

For example, when I set out to write my first book, I wanted to feel credible (a desire likely shared by most first-time writers). So I got clear on why I wanted to feel that way: so that people would read my books, trust the message within, and I could truly help as many people as possible. I set my plan and actions. I never for a second even contemplated winning big fancy awards. I was just focused on getting through the 'doing'. Word by word, paragraph by paragraph, page by page. I made my plan, surrendered to the process and immersed myself in action. Less than a year later, the Universe had rewarded my efforts. In abundance. It's just one example of how, when you decide to let your Soul-self lead your life from your heart – and you spend as much time *doing* as you do *dreaming* – the most amazing things can happen.

So this chapter is about unlocking your full potential. Taking control of your life, with grace and with love. Creating the future that resonates with who you really are. Allowing yourself to expand and step ever closer to your purpose.

It's simple to achieve. Know who you are. Then get practical about making choices and decisions that honour you.

Every day you will do this a little more, then a little more, and with each day lived more in sync with who you really are, you say yes to your Soul-self. You open yourself up to beauty. You live your purpose. You experience blissful Soul happiness.

Creation follows intention

Creating the life of your dreams is simple. All you have to do is understand the creation cycle that is innately part of all of us, and apply it in your life.

The cycle forces clarity. It demands action. But you know what? Routinely apply this wisdom with the intention of being your Soul-self in every part of your life, and your outer life and your inner self will effortlessly mirror one another.

There's a very good reason for that. Creation follows intention. This law applies to absolutely anything in the world, and anything in your life. Like, growing a vegetable garden. Building a house. Conceiving a child. Getting a new job. Writing a book. Taking a holiday.

First you have to want it, and know why. Then you have to make choices and do some planning. And then you have to nurture it with positive focus. And finally you give it form with action, manifestation or expression.

The four stages of the creation cycle are:

- **Desire.** Desire is about having the intention, wish, thought, idea, need, vision. This intention is the source of all creation.
- **Direction.** Direction is about following intention with order, planning, decisions, choices, design. It is about knowing what needs to be done.
- **Dedication.** Dedication brings in focus through nurturing, love, process, positivity, attention. It is bringing intention into being.
- **Doing.** Doing is about creating the desired outcome through manifestation, expression, action, production. It is about completing the cycle.

I love gardening, so let's use a gardening example to help explain this cycle further. To create a garden, first you have to want to. You have the idea, or the intention and you know why you want it. To grow nutritious, organic vegetables, or to delight in beautiful flowering blooms, for example. This is the *Desire*. Then you must decide what to plant and where. You need to know what supplies you need and where you will get them from. This is the *Direction*. Then you need to give focused attention to your idea. You probably visualise your beautiful, productive garden. You start researching recipes for utilising the produce you will harvest. And you start nurturing and preparing the garden bed. This is the *Dedication*. Then comes the time for the *Doing*. You need to plant the seedlings and bring your original intention into being. And the cycle doesn't stop there. You want to produce a bountiful crop (Desire), so you decide the steps you need to take (Direction), you take those steps like weeding, watering and fertilising to support your garden (Dedication), and you reap the rewards harvesting fresh juicy vegetables and aromatic herbs (Doing).

Whenever I have a desire that resonates with my Soul-self and my purpose, I take the time to get really clear about it and to map it out. I like bringing my ideas into reality. And you know what? Every time I follow the creation process, what I desire happens. Sometimes like magic.

And here's why: this cycle is innately part of life, and of us. Our lives are continually going through these four stages, and you can harness the creative power of that cycle in your own life.

All the insights you had in Part One of this book are essential. Without them, you can still use the creation process – it's naturally occurring – but your mind-self will be leading the way, charging ahead in the direction it wants to go without first understanding your deeper *why*.

That is the beauty of dreaming. You give yourself permission to be, and you set the context for the rest of your life. You are the reason. Your Soul is the calling. Soul happiness is the context.

The art of intention

So, once you feel like you clearly know your Soul-self, and you have created your Soul map, how do you know what you really want next? And how do you know that it is in alignment with who you really are?

That's where your desires, your deepest feelings, the whispers of your heart come in. It's also where practicality comes in. You need to balance the two to create the life you want and a life that resonates with who you are.

At this point, you may be tempted to skip the first part of the creation process, Desire, in favour of skipping straight to the planning aspect of Direction. But really, you have to know why you want the things you want before you can be sure the choices you are making are the right ones.

And to get clarity you need intention. You have to begin with the end in mind, and ultimately know how you want to feel in your life.

Your Soul map will be an anchor for your intention. It provides the framework, sets the higher direction. But you still need to distil your purpose and all your dreams into achievable chunks.

I'm a fan of intentions rather than goals, and the difference is quite distinct. Intentions link you to your Soul. They reflect what is in your heart, who you are and what you value. Whereas goals are usually outside of us, external to our being.

It's only once you have your intentions set that goals or objectives then have their place. They're explicit, and help you manifest your intentions in tangible ways. The goals are the things you tick off your 'list'. But they are infinitely more powerful when you connect with your deepest intentions and desires first.

The synergetic relationship between intentions and goals is akin to that between inspiration and motivation. Inspiration is the spark, the seed, the vision from within. Motivation is about tangible action, the impetus to get things done. Inspiration is heart-based rather than head-based. It draws things towards you.

Without inspiration, motivation feels like a Soulless push. Combine the two and magic happens.

So, let's say my intention is to have a deeper level of self-care, because when I am balanced I am naturally connected to my guidance. And that inspires me. One of the goals I could set for that intention would be to practice yoga more consistently. The objective might then be to go to at least three yoga classes a week. That motivates me.

By being clear about my intention, I've really connected with my deepest desires for myself and my life. It makes me prioritise going to that yoga class. I could simply have the goal of doing more yoga. But without understanding why I want to (the intention), or exactly how I'm going to (the objective), the goal lacks Soul.

When you release the need for checks and ticks and instead focus on feelings, you allow yourself to become self-full. By becoming self-full we naturally become Soulful. The whole process is a balance: you need to have your deepest dreams, intentions and desires, but then you need to get real about getting things done. Which is why we add the focus, the action, the goals and the objectives. That's how you manifest anything you want in life. It's about the dreaming and the doing.

Soulful goals

You need to dive deep into why you want what you want. What really underlies that wanting? When you combine your intention with goals, you sustain your spirit, gain clarity and focus, understand who you truly are and step ever closer to your shining self.

This is why, when we attain our wildly successful careers we still feel empty. Yes, our career may leave us feeling recognised, or proud, or powerful, or independent. But is that really what we desire in life? Perhaps instead of feeling recognised, we really want to feel *valued*. Instead of proud we want to feel *fulfilled*. Instead of powerful we want to feel *bold*. Instead of independent we want to feel *free*. The career gives us an aspect of those feelings, but it doesn't quite hit the mark, because our choices have been attainment driven rather than focused on feelings.

Remember, your feelings are your inbuilt compass for everything in life. Your feelings are your true north. They connect you to your spirit. Instead of focusing on what you want to do and have and achieve, focus on how you want to feel. This is the truest way to honour your spirit and to connect to the path of your purpose.

I'm not saying that having goals and getting results is a worthless exercise. Far from it. But goals with Soul get even greater results. It's just a case of flipping the goal setting process on its head. So reach for whatever your heart desires. The keys are: know why you want it, want it with all your heart, but release the attachment to getting it.

You know you've got your priorities right when you want to feel free more than you want to please other people, or you want to feel beautiful more than you want to look beautiful, or you want to feel self-love more than you want to chase love, or you want to feel empowered more than you want to tick accomplishments off your list. These are Soul priorities, the kind that will keep filling your heart and your life with more and more gifts. Soul priorities fulfil Soul purpose.

We can become very fixated on our goals in life. Married by 25. Children by 30. Earning $100,000 by 35. Holiday home by 40. Mortgage free by 45. Retired by 50. Then you can start living. The thing to understand is what do you really love about those goals? How will they make you feel? Is that what you want or need to feel? This sort of goal planning in life is very fixed and rigid. And most likely doesn't honour who you really are.

When it comes to being in Soul flow, you need to move away from having fixed goals. They only constrict your spirit, create an enormous amount of pressure, and ultimately limit the gifts that are waiting for you.

In the scenario above, what if you had followed your heart and established your own technology company in your parent's spare room at age 21? You could have made your first $100,000 in a year, been a multi-millionaire by 25, established a charitable trust to make technology available to underprivileged kids by 28, and been able to retire by 30, meet your future husband and travel the world doing humanitarian work with children.

When you follow your heart, trust your intuition, but bring your head with you too, you create a world of possibility in your life.

Perhaps it's more useful to look at it in this way. Instead of fixed goals, there are things you'd love to happen in life. And then have the intention to fulfil those desires. Just do what you love. In one way or another. And the rest will come. Release the need to force or control or dictate anything. Focus on the joy of saying yes to your spirit.

The easiest way to follow your heart is to detach from the outcome. Even the wisest philosophers, the most savvy business people, the most enlightened spiritual teachers still ground their intuition. They wait for clarity. They act when the time is right. They rarely make hasty decisions. They don't assume they can see the whole picture by themselves. They seek advice or direction, knowing that even teachers remain students.

To reflect this type of approach in your own life, ask yourself these questions about your goals and desires. *How strong are my expectations? How attached am I to this outcome? If things changed, could I let go of the need for this tomorrow?*

This is the reason why inner purpose is so important. Life is constantly unfolding before us. From moment to moment, you never know what will happen next. Life can be turned upside down in an instant. You could be following your heart and be completely on path with your outer purpose and still it could change overnight. And you would still have a choice as to what to do, and how you would wake up and take new steps the next day. When you really think about it, it's an undeniable and humbling privilege to even have the chance to follow your heart. You and I are not among the millions and millions of people enslaved worldwide. We have freedom to choose. And that is worth some serious gratitude. So, when you are centred in your true self you are able to flow with change and be content in almost any circumstances. That's why inner purpose is essential for outer purpose. And why Soulful goals will keep you focused on what's true in your life.

Your time is now

Danielle La Porte says, "Small deliberate actions inspired by your true desires create a life you love."

You can dream and desire and plan all you like. But unless you take action, unless you commit to doing the things you need to do to feel the way you want to feel, and be who you want to be… Nothing. I repeat, gorgeous – nothing will change.

It goes back to that little thing called freewill. You have choice. And not only do you have to decide how you want your life to be, you have to decide to make it so.

Stop yourself right here. I know what you're thinking. *It's too late. I'm too old. There's not enough time. I can't possibly do this. I must be making this up. Why have I only just realised this now? Why has life spun me in the way it has. This isn't how it's meant to be, surely. I'm not really that special… or important… or worthy.*

Well, beautiful you. Let me stop you right there. First of all, tame those thoughts! Then, know two things. Firstly, everything in your life has been leading you to this point – the lessons you have learnt, the timing of events, the people you have encountered – it has all been part of this gorgeous picture that *you* have created for yourself. And secondly, know you have a choice. You can keep on the same path. Or, you can commit to the beautiful dreams you have and start living your purpose a little bit more every day, remembering all the while that this is what you had planned all along.

Don't let your mind make this bigger than it needs to be. It doesn't have to be an overnight transformation. This isn't about turning your life upside down – unless that's what you want to do. It's about honouring how you feel. When you do, everything falls into place. When you get clear on what you really desire for yourself, you have choice. And you can choose to make changes, big or small, to your being and your life, every day. It's about baby steps. Doing something – even just one thing every day or every week or every month – that takes you closer to your dream. Every choice takes you closer to who you are – your Soul-self – and closer to your purpose and the life of your dreams.

Now is perfect. Now is the right time, the best time, and the only time you have to truly live your life in sync with your Soul.

Infuse your life with purpose

Here's the thing: Soul purpose is about having purpose in *every* part of your life. That's why, throughout this book, I guide you to consider every part of your life as a whole – mind, body, emotion and spirit. When you have purpose in every part of your life, it naturally becomes easier to align to a higher purpose.

But maybe you feel like you don't have a higher purpose. That's ok. Completely. Even if you feel like your purpose is simply to be a good person that brings joy to others, you can align every part of your life to that purpose. It is not just one aspect of you. Purpose underlies everything we do.

Here is a four-step approach to ensuring you have purpose in every part of your life. This whole process links beautifully with your Soul map. It helps you to keep your life and yourself aligned with your Soulful values and intentions. For deeper guidance on this part, see the Soul Happiness companion workbook available at **www.marniemcdermott.com**

1. Understand the links between each area of your life

You've probably heard the term 'life balance'. It generally refers to bringing a harmony and equal priority to every part of your life. Life coaches will talk about key areas of your life as career, finances, relationships, home, family, recreation, health, wellbeing, leisure, for example. But just as there are four key aspects to who we are – mind, body, emotion and spirit, and four key elements in the creation cycle – desire, direction, dedication and doing, I also believe there are four areas of our life. And you have encountered them already in this book.

When thinking about bringing your inner and outer life into harmony, I guide you to see your life as these four distinct areas:

- *Purpose + Spirit.* Linked to the spiritual aspect of our being, this relates to our deepest self. It's about your deepest acceptance of yourself. Your own Soulful beliefs and practices. It's about who you are.

- *Lifestyle + Living.* Linked to the mind level of our being, this relates to all aspects of your career and finances, education, and lifestyle factors like your home, possessions and travel. It's about what you do and what you have.

- *Love + Relationships.* Linked to the emotional aspect of our being, this is about the love in your life. Love for others, love for your community, causes, the planet. It is about your passions, creativity and expression.

- *Health + Wellbeing.* Linked to the physical level of our being, this is about your health, nutrition, self-care, as well as leisure activities, hobbies and relaxation. It's about how you nurture yourself.

So your Soul map from Chapter 7 provides the higher, wider context for your life. And these four life areas allow you to filter your highest purpose, values and intentions through every area of your life.

Within each of these four aspects of your life, you bring yourself into greater harmony and alignment with your purpose when you understand how you want to feel in each area. Decide what's important, then identify how you want to *feel* so you know what you need to *do*.

2. Take time to reflect

So, how do you know how you want to feel in each area of your life?

There's an old adage that says "to know where you're going, you have to know where you've been". In other words, to know what you want or how you want to feel, you have to know how you feel right now. You need a point of reference or a benchmark. That's where reflection comes in.

Reflection is easy. Again, it just takes time. You've probably been doing a lot of reflection throughout this book already. It's especially useful for allowing your own guidance and intuition to surface.

Reflection is like evaluation. But evaluation with Soul and feeling. There are many ways to use reflection. Here's one: take each of the four life areas, and then think about the last year of your life. Write down what the year has brought you in each area. This is more than just creating a list of achievements. You want to go deeper and understand the significance of things that happened. Understand how you feel in each area. What you have experienced. What you have learnt. So, less of the neatly-packaged evaluation one might find in a workplace. And more of the Soul-satisfying reflection that dives deep to your core.

The difference between reflection and evaluation is like the difference between mindlessly ticking things off your 'list', and appreciating the deeper Soulful experiences you have had. It's like, you may tick off going back to school and obtaining your degree. Great achievement. But on deeper reflection, you would see the expansiveness of this experience – your deeper sense of self, the deeply held patterns you have shifted around feeling worthy, the joy of believing in yourself.

You could also look at each of the four life areas and ask yourself:

- How do I feel right now in this area of my life? Where am I at?
- What do I need to release? What's not working and what do I need to let go?
- What do I love? What am I grateful for? What do I need to value more?
- What do I want to welcome in? What do I need to change, do differently, create space for, start doing?

3. Create your Soulful life plan

You've created your Soul map. Now it's time to filter that down further and really align your inner and outer worlds by creating your life map.

Remember, it's the plan, the blueprint for creating the life you want.

You've established what is important to you within each of the four life areas and reflected on them.

Now you need to allow yourself time. Take a full day or longer to create your Soulful life plan. Spend time dreaming of your beautiful life, and write it down. Have four major intentions or goals for the year. One in each key area of your life. No more.

Remember to express these as "I am" statements to really anchor them.

You may even like to set a life theme for the year. For example, after spending three months travelling last year, the theme for me this year was 'consolidation'. The year I consolidated. You could have more than one theme.

Then, using your reflection as a guide:

- Know what's important – what are your priorities?
- Decide how to make it happen – make specific promises to yourself.
- Take action – break it down into bite-sized steps. What's one thing, just one, that could take you closer to where you want to be?

Once you've completed your plan, take a break. Allow the ideas, the awareness, the beauty of what you've created to infuse your heart and your whole being. Come back to it in a few days. Check in. What's changed? What feels even clearer now?

Refine it. Then start doing it. Remember, it's up to you. This is how you create your reality. You will end up with a really simple plan that may look a little like this:

MY SOULFUL LIFE PLAN			
Purpose + Spirit I am:	Lifestyle + Living I am:	Love + Relationships I am:	Health + Wellbeing I am:
My one key thing:	My one key thing:	My one key thing:	My one key thing:
MY THEME FOR THE YEAR			

4. Keep focused

To get serious about getting into Soul flow, you need to have – and it's one of my favourites – order.

Order helps everything flow, and it helps you keep focused. And a plan is worthless if you never do anything with it.

Here's a Soulful planning framework that I suggest for bringing order and flow to your life.

Yearly: DREAM	Plan an annual soulful retreat for getting crystal clear clarity on your dreams and desires, and creating your plan for the year.
Quarterly: CHECK-IN	Have a mini retreat every quarter to pause, reconnect, refocus and keep in flow.
Monthly: PLAN	Map out the month ahead. Know what you need to do (actions), and when you need to do it by (timeframes).
Weekly: ACT	Plan the week ahead. Bring dreams into being with simple, achievable, bite-sized steps.

Daily:	Try a daily intention or mini mantra to keep you focused on
FOCUS	how you want to feel, or what you want to achieve.

Bringing order to creating the life you want harnesses and programmes your mind to live in tune with the true you. Your Soul-self is so infinite it can be and do anything when it is honoured, it all depends on your thoughts and your intention.

I have always been a fan of planning and lists. Of working out what I want, and how I'm going to get there. That's my thing, and I understand that it may not be yours. But the one thing you need to appreciate, the new way of being you need to embrace, is that if you stay where you are, you are not going to get where you want to go.

You've already glimpsed where that is. You've got a deeper understanding of your Soul code, perhaps you've even been doing the exercises and you have already created your Soul map too. This is your inner self, your Soul-self, your being. This chapter is going to help you bring more of the true you – your dreams, wishes and deepest desires – into your life. Just as the previous chapter was about helping you to understand, at the deepest level, who you are; this chapter is about giving you the tools to align your outer life with your inner self. In other words, to make sure your life reflects who you truly are.

I've learnt that you have to anchor your desires in a practical way. Life is so busy, that you need clarity to stay focused and on track. Clarity comes not when you let things float around in your head, become overwhelming or consuming, or able to float off, forever forgotten. Clarity comes when you anchor all those gorgeous dreams and wishes in a very tangible way. In writing.

Simple reflection

This chapter has guided you to consider the four key aspects of your life, and to understand how you bring the dreams you have for yourself into alignment with your purpose using your Soul map as the key.

Turn to a new page in your journal, or the relevant page in the Soul Happiness companion workbook.

Creation cycles

- Think about the four stages of the creation cycle – Desire. Direction. Dedication. Doing. Consider how you could apply those to a task, project, or dream you have right now.

- Consider some of the key goals or desires you have in your life right now. Ask yourself: *How strong are my expectations? How attached am I to this outcome? If things changed, could I let go of the need for this tomorrow?*

Soulful life planning

- Turn to a new page in your journal, or the relevant page in the Soul Happiness companion workbook.

- Revisit your Soul map from Chapter 7. Have your highest intentions and desires for your life front of mind.

- Draw four boxes on the page, or use four separate pages if you want more space, one for each life area: purpose + spirit, lifestyle + living, love + relationships, health + wellbeing.

- For each area, first be grateful for what you love in each area of your life. What's working. And be aware of what is no longer serving you and needs to change. Then write your beautiful life story in each area. Your wishes for your life in the next year. Check-in. How do these dreams support your Soul map?

- Then for each life area, summarise your dreams with just one intention or goal. Start each statement with "I am", as though everything you want is already real.

- For each area, decide on a priority action that will take you closer to your dream. Just one key thing.

- Once you've completed your plan, take a break. Allow the ideas, the awareness, the beauty of what you've created to infuse your heart and your whole being.

- Come back to it in a few days. Check in. What's changed? What feels even clearer now? Refine it.

- Break your intentions and goals into bite-sized chunks, then start doing it.

- Use the Soulful planning framework on pages 139-140 to keep focused throughout the year.

- Add your Soulful life plan to your Soul map to have the total picture of your intention and desires. It may look like this:

MY SOUL MAP

GUIDING PRINCIPLES:	OUTER PURPOSE:
• Purpose + Spirit: • Lifestyle + Living: • Love + Relationships: • Health + Wellbeing:	
INNER FOCUS:	**SOUL CHARACTER:** Inner: Outer:

MY SOULFUL LIFE PLAN

Purpose + Spirit I am:	Lifestyle + Living I am:	Love + Relationships I am:	Health + Wellbeing I am:
My one key thing:	My one key thing:	My one key thing:	My one key thing:

MY THEME FOR THE YEAR

.... ❧ ....

Simple promise

Make this simple promise to yourself now. Remind yourself of this promise throughout your day or write it down where you will see it.

I take action to create my beautiful life.

Simple practices

These simple steps can help you put the ideas in this chapter into practice. Remember, there is power in doing something. Anything. Just one thing. Because the moment you do, you make a conscious change in your life.

Balance. The key to all planning is balance. Make sure you schedule time for the things that are important to you.

Keep inspiration where you can see it. Breathe life into your dreams and desires for your life. Declare them. Write them down. Use a vision board or create a Pinterest board.

Have good habits. Creating the life you really want is as much about dreaming as doing. Be mindful of creation cycles and commit to an annual Soulful planning approach.

Live your priorities. Take the time to know what you want to avoid. You don't want to wake up one day to discover you've been living for other people's priorities.

Plan. Remember, if you don't have a plan for your life, someone else does! Take charge and allow yourself to naturally get into Soul flow.

CHAPTER 9

secret 9: manifest your dreams

If you dwell in abundance you will have abundance.
~ Marianne Williamson

A key secret of being in Soul flow is knowing how to manifest your dreams. This chapter will help you understand the principles of manifestation and how you can apply them in your life.

My very first experience of wishing something with all my heart and having it come true was when I was about 11 years old.

My little country school had an annual agricultural day. The kind where students would rear an animal – like a calf, lamb or kid (baby goat) – and then 'show' that pet for judging. All your hard work came down to a single day. You would lead your pet. You would call your pet so it came to you. You would be judged on how well groomed your pet was and how it looked.

It was a fierce competition, with the coveted prizes being the junior and senior 'calf club cup'.

I had won the senior calf club cup the year before. I was proud as punch. But I wanted more. Even at that young age I had ambition, a desire to do better, to excel.

It was my last year at primary school, my last ever calf club and I desperately wanted to win the senior calf club cup for the second year running.

But my aspirations didn't stop there. The school's annual flower show happened on the same day and to have a decent chance at winning, you had to enter artistic floral interpretations in several categories.

I wanted to win the senior flower show cup too. A clean sweep. Both cups. Because no one ever had.

And so, in the months and weeks before the year's annual competition, my 11-year-old self was ramping up my usual nightly talks with God and making a bit of a deal.

It went a little like this.

> *Dear God, if you're listening, I really want to win the senior calf club cup AND the senior flower show cup. I want to win them both so that Mum and Dad are proud of me. Could you make that happen? Pleeeeeaaassssee? If you let me win I promise I will stop biting my nails. Forever. Thank you. I love you.*

I was in full manifestation mode. Of course I had no idea that's what I was doing, nor that I was applying all the principles of manifestation. Innately. I was tapping into the source of infinite possibility we all draw from long before I even knew what it was.

Every night I was visualising what I wanted, and declaring it (I used to talk out loud as I lay in bed before sleep). I would often daydream it too. My intention for what I wanted was crystal clear.

You'd think that I would have become obsessed with spending more time with my calf, Daisy. But no. It seems that I also naturally applied one of the other rules of manifesting – I did my part, but I also detached and let go.

I did the minimum I had to. I fed Daisy, twice a day. I trained her to walk on a lead. I brushed her. We hung out.

At times I was resentful at Mum's prodding that I spend more time with Daisy. You see, I knew God had it in hand. And as long as I believed that, it would happen. I would win. And no amount of extra time or effort I put in would make a single bit of difference.

Besides, Daisy and I had a pretty special bond. I understood her, and she understood me perfectly too.

The big day finally came around. I was up early making my flower creations. Daisy was fed and brushed until her coat gleamed. And God held up her end of the bargain. I won. Both cups.

There's a photo of me. I'm sitting on my bed wearing a teal-coloured knit tracksuit proudly displaying my cups and all my individual prize ribbons. I look a little quizzical. Maybe because I thought other people's pets were better than mine, and other people's floral art looked better than mine. But, really I wasn't surprised. Because I got exactly what I asked for.

Oh, and I stopped biting my nails too. Just like I promised. I'd tried stopping so many times before. I'd been bribed countless times with thoughts of all the pretty nail polishes I could have if only I had long nails. And I'd been grossed out by that yucky tasting stuff Mum made me paint on my nails as a deterrent from biting them. Yet I kept on biting them regardless.

But this time, quitting being a nail-biter was easy because I had a promise to keep. It happened overnight because, not only had I spent all that time manifesting a double-cup win, I'd spent all that time manifesting beautiful nails too. I haven't bitten my nails since.

Since then I've manifested all sorts of things in my life. I've learnt that I get what I ask for. Dream homes. Perfect jobs. Pay rises. Jet-setting corporate travel. Money. House sales. Meetings with spiritual teachers. Soul love. Book awards. Car parks. Clothing in my size and on sale.

And every time I followed that same process my 11-year-old self mastered. Back then I knew what I wanted. I knew why I wanted it. I truly wanted it with all my heart. I did what I could do. And I let go of everything else.

I'm going to walk you through that exact process in this chapter. But first, let's understand some basic principles that underpin successful manifestation.

You can manifest whatever you want

Here's the first thing you need to understand. Manifestation is not just for the highly spiritual.

My 11-year-old self was hardly a spiritual guru able to pull gems from thin air. I was just a normal kid with a heartfelt desire.

You are exactly the same. Right now you have the power to create whatever you want in your life. The clearer you are about what you want, the more you have the power to pull it into your life.

For years I was a serial ditherer. Indecisive. Scared to make the wrong decision. Heck, any decision. And if I made a decision, you can be sure I changed my mind. The problem is that's just sending out mixed messages to the Universe. And that's how we end up stuck in place. Feeling frustrated. And like things never seem to work out how we want them to.

The bottom line is, nothing happens until you decide what you want.

Think of it like this. If the Universe was a takeaway store and you were standing at the counter, you need to place a precise order. You can't stand there indecisive about what you feel like eating. Nothing happens until you place an order. And in a real-life takeaway store you usually don't say, "I don't know what I want, but here's five bucks. Just give me anything."

And if you decide you want a burger, well you get pretty specific about the kind of burger you want to order too. In my case, *A falafel burger on a gluten-free bun and hold the pickles, please.* Now that's specific.

In the kitchen of that Universal takeaway store, your Soul team springs into action, whipping up the fulfilment of your order and usually bringing you something more than you asked for too.

I like to call it 'cosmic ordering'. Be clear. Be specific. And, if it is for your highest good, you will get all you desire or perhaps even something better.

So tell the Universe what you desire (all the tools in this book will help you get clear on that). Know why you want it. Place your order. Release the need to control the outcome. And watch what happens. Our thoughts and feelings programme our reality. And just like any computer programme, the Universe recalculates and recalibrates itself based on the programme or the script you are writing. The Universe delivers what you ask for. Precisely. So be clear about what you want and why.

You can have so much fun with this too. Start experimenting a little even now. I often ask and receive the perfect car parking space, complete with pre-paid time on the meter. It's true. Even with this practice I notice that the more clear I am with my intention, the better the result. For example, if I just ask for a space with money on the meter – I find that when I park up, get out of my car and look at how much time is left on the parking meter there may only be five minutes. However, if I am specific and say something like 'at least 30 minutes' or '30 minutes or more' then that's what I get. Thirty minutes. Sometimes forty. Sometimes more. Because I haven't limited it. I've said what I'd like, but I've left it open to receive something better too. I do this also with clothes or things I would like for myself. For example, I may see a top that I love but I don't have the money for it at that precise moment. In cases like this, I always place an order for the top to be available in my size and on sale when I return to the store. If I really love the top, it will be there, in my size, on sale, sometimes months later. When I don't do this and buy an item then and there at full price, the next time I'm in the store, sure enough, there it is, in my size, *on sale!*

We live in a material world for a reason

It's ok to want good things. Soulful living isn't about wanting less. You are a spiritual being in a material world. There are two reasons for that.

Firstly, because you need to master detachment from things and realise that your worth, your identity, your wealth, and most certainly your happiness do not come from those things.

And secondly, because you are here to learn to manifest all you desire. To live the life you want. To become limitless. To fulfil your potential. By mastering the laws of creation. You are here to learn that you can create exactly what you want for yourself and to realise that you've been doing that your whole life.

Many people see a contradiction with spiritual ideas and spiritual laws being used to create abundance and prosperity and to make dreams come true. I say that is exactly why we live in a material world. One of our lessons is to master thoughts and intentions.

Yearn for greatness! It's ok to want good things for ourselves and to believe we are special. Simply because we are talking about Soul or spiritual purpose does not mean you need to resign yourself to being a spiritually-awake pauper. It's ok to desire comfort and security, and a lovely home and a steady flow of prosperity, or whatever it is you desire for yourself. Material wanting is ok. The secret is to release the need for it. Have the intention for what you want in life. But detach from *having* to have it. Then you'll receive it and more.

The simple truth is, the more aligned your inner and outer lives are – with your inner purpose being expressed authentically in your outer life – and the more you believe and trust and allow yourself to grow, the more abundance will flow to you.

As part of your inner purpose you may find yourself confronted with a lesson of 'lack', which may be blocking the flow of abundance in your life. That lack mentality or belief may see you feel fearful of not having enough of everything – money, love, friends, experiences, belongings. This translates into outer experiences where you struggle to make ends meet, you may be made redundant, or you could lose your possessions or livelihood.

Abundance and prosperity are your natural right. The only thing that blocks it now is something within you. Aligning your outer world with your deepest desires and truths will allow the flow to be even greater.

What you receive is based on what you believe

You need to understand that your reality is based on what you believe is possible.

So if you believe black cars are sexier than silver cars, you'll see more black cars than silver. It doesn't mean there's less silver cars out there, just that you've trained yourself to see black cars.

Similarly, if you believe that everyone else in your team at work is more senior, knowledgeable and capable than you; you will most likely be overlooked for opportunities and career progression.

And, if you tolerate less than desirable behaviour because you believe your husband, partner, boyfriend or significant other is the best you're ever going to get, that behaviour will only get worse.

Belief is everything. And as I talked about in chapter 3, most of the beliefs we carry around about ourselves and our life are false. They aren't our own truth.

Our beliefs limit us. I used to think that chocolate anything was the best flavour in the world. Chocolate bars. Chocolate ice cream. Chocolate cake. I would choose the same thing, time and time again, ignoring every other option. In every ice cream parlour or bakery or on every dessert menu, I honed in only on chocolate. I wasn't consciously aware of the myriad of other flavours, options and combinations because in my mind, chocolate was the only thing I liked. I believed I only liked chocolate, so chocolate was all I ever looked for and chocolate was all I ever saw. The fact is, these days there are so many other things I prefer to chocolate. And when I opened my mind to new possibilities, suddenly the world was filled with amazing options that blew my mind. Like delightfully delicate blueberry vegan cheesecake. Sticky, gooey apricot and coconut bliss balls. And the pure, unadulterated joy of my homemade strawberry ice cream. All animal-friendly of course!

It's a simple metaphor I know. But so many of us live our lives like that. Our beliefs cause us to have very limited views about what is possible. And if you can't see something for yourself, like my inability to see past chocolate on any menu, then you simply can't have it.

When you expand your horizons and step out of your comfort zone in any aspect of your life, you open yourself up to more than just chocolate. The possibilities you can create in your life are endless, and manifestation is simply that. Understanding infinite possibility.

The biggest block is your inner balance

Now I'm not a quantum physicist, or in any way scientifically minded. But science has proved that there is an invisible energy realm that creates everything, connects everything and governs everything. You can call it what you will – God, Source, Prana, Chi, the Universe, or the field of potentiality (as Deepak Chopra calls it). In her book E^2 Pam Grout likens it to the 'force' of Star Wars movie fame. It is within us, all around us. I call it the 'infinite field of love'. Everything grows from love.

Whether you know it or not, you are part of that energy. You are energy. Everything in your life, everything on the planet – living and breathing or not – and everything in the whole Universe is energy. That energy grows things, fixes things, and constantly works to purify everything. Its basis is wholeness and balance.

Manifestation is about being in balance. When your inner belief is aligned with your outer desire, you can have anything you want.

But so often, on the inside, we question, we second guess, we believe we don't deserve it. Even though we really want it, we feel like we're not good enough.

Think of it like this. It's like you are a gigantic magnet, pulling stuff towards you. That stuff can be good or not so good, depending on what you think, what you believe and what you will allow for yourself.

The purity of that magnet is determined by the health of your energy field or aura. And when you feel out of balance and not in alignment, it's always because part of your energy field is also out of balance.

Energetic imbalance caused by mental, emotional and spiritual blocks, stops the pulling power of your inner manifestation magnet.

Your solar plexus is your energy centre and uses its pulling power to reel in the desires of the sacral chakra, your creative centre. So, balance your chakras and your energy field regularly. When you keep them bright and clear, your manifestation ability also amplifies.

Manifestation is simply transforming energy into form. So when your energy is clear – when you're balanced and centred, feeling connected and have crystal clear intention for what you want in your life – can you imagine how strong the pulling power of your manifestation magnet would be? Intense.

I notice that when I'm not centred and connected within myself, when I let questioning and overwhelm creep in, it's like the Universal takeaway store gets confused too. Because I'm muddled, it doesn't know what to do. So everything comes to a halt. Business may get a bit slow. Payments are missed. Multiple light bulbs will blow. Time seems lacking rather than abundant. It's times like this that taking a day off to refocus and rebalance is essential. It's like a system reboot. Then everything can fall back into rhythm and harmony once more.

The art of manifesting

When thinking about manifestation, most people generally think it's about vision boards and affirmations. They have their place, absolutely. But there is so much more.

These are the steps to successful manifestation.

Create space for the new

First, you have to create room in your life for what you want. To welcome goodness into your life, you must create the space for it.

You need space to grow. Space for your Soul to expand. Space for gifts to be received, wishes to be answered, dreams to breathe.

You can create space in your life in several ways.

- **Clear clutter.** Clutter blocks the flow in our life. Manifestation is the flow of energy into our life based on our intentions. The flow is how everything we want travels to us. It's like the sea is to a ship. So, spring clean your life inside and out. The more you clear clutter, the faster the flow of goodness in your life will be. For more tips on order and flow, see Chapter 4 in *Beyond Happiness*.

- **Give thanks.** The more grateful we are for all that we have, the more we open ourselves to receive. A grateful heart creates a grateful mind, and a grateful mind sees boundless possibilities. When you are grateful, you always get more than you expect. For more tips on gratitude, see Chapter 6 in *Beyond Happiness*.

- **Let go.** Sometimes there are things – situations, people, events, and more – that we just have to let go of because they create mental or emotional clutter in our lives. The more we hold on to, the less space we have for happiness. For more tips on emotional and mental clutter clearing, see Chapters 5 and 10 in *Beyond Happiness*.

Know what you want and why

Ultimately the reason we want anything is because of how we want to feel. And it's ok to want what feels good, whatever that may be for you. Just be sure you know why you want it, and that it's your story you are writing, not someone else's. It's easy to get caught up in the storybook happiness trap, basing your ideals of happiness on your perceptions of other people's lives. Their story is different, their path is different, their life is different. So their notion of 'having it all' will be different. So, want what you want. Have desires. Enjoy nice things. But always live your own life and not someone else's.

Once you know what you want and why, declare it. Some of us hope, wish, dream and never get any further. The key is to decide. To speak it out loud. To write it down. To place your order. To anchor your desires.

Remember to be specific. Be detailed about what you want. Remember to take the boundaries off what is possible and dream big. It's okay to upsize your takeaway order!

Once you've asked for what you want, expect delivery. Don't worry about how it will happen – you're not in charge of the how. Just know that the Universe will do what's needed to be done to deliver your dreams to you.

Make a choice

The decisions you make in every moment create your life. Dreams become reality because you make a choice. That choice involves action. It involves doing something, one thing, every day that takes you closer to where you want to be. Expect to have to do something to bring you into alignment for manifesting all you want. For example, I needed to trust my repetitive thoughts about entering selected book awards in order to receive the wins I did. If I'd decided not to, I would have blocked the flow of all that was being bought to me. You always have to hold up your end of the bargain and it always involves real life steps and courage to trust your intuition.

Believe

The Universe loves bringing us gifts, big and small. It's a reminder of how treasured, special and loved you are. You can have whatever you desire. You simply have to believe you deserve it and be completely open to receiving it. And the more on purpose you are, the more rewarded you will be. Every time I trust how I feel and reflect that trust in a decision around my business, I am rewarded. More customers. More glowing feedback. More income. The opportunity to do more good. When you have discovered your own inner rewards, the outer rewards only get bigger.

Do what you love without attachment

Usually the things you want never happen how you expect, or how you plan. Quite possibly the only difference between getting exactly what you want, or not, is your level of attachment to getting it. This is the Law of Attraction at its finest. Match your intentions and your thoughts to what it is you want to receive, and then let go of all attachment to the outcome. Then you shall receive.

But when you are attached to the outcome of a situation, desperately wanting it to happen in a certain way, you do two things. Firstly, you create resistance. Over planning seeks to control the outcome. Control creates resistance. Resistance repels the very thing you desire. Secondly, you place very defined limits on your order. The truth is the Universe may wish to bring you something more.

When you have the intention and create the space for it to be filled, you open yourself to receive. So there's a big difference between desperately wanting and hoping something will happen, and loving it to happen. Want is constricting. Love is expansive.

To bring your dreams to life, be clear about your desires and passions in each area of your life, detach from any need or greed, and commit to positive action that honours your spirit.

The ultimate manifestation secret

You can take all the steps I've outlined in this chapter and still block everything you desire. And there's a simple reason for that. In fact, it's the biggest secret to manifesting anything you desire, whether it's love, happiness, abundance, whatever.

The secret is *alignment*. And it's a not-so-secret theme in this book. When you align your inner and outer worlds, you also align your inner and outer self. It's like the inner and outer are talking the same language, watching the same channel, singing the same tune. The inner and the outer get in flow. And miracles happen when there is alignment.

So, set your deepest intentions for your life and then align with them. Heart and mind. Body and Soul. Inner and outer. Walk the talk. Decide you deserve this goodness. And watch it bloom.

You can gauge your alignment by noticing what happens in your heart (feelings) and your mind (thoughts) when you think about your dreamiest intentions and goals. Do the actions in your life say 'I want this'? How can you align your head and your heart with your desires?

Aligning the inner and the outer is like syncing the dreaming with the doing. When you do that, you attract all the creative forces of the Universe and anything becomes possible.

Allow yourself to express who you truly are in the world and prepare to be delighted, amazed and blessed. Soul flow is inevitable.

.... ❊ ....

Simple reflection

Knowing how to manifest your dreams is both a skill and an art and this reflection will guide you to open up to using it more consciously in your life.

In a new page in your journal, or on the relevant page in your Soul Happiness companion workbook, consider the following questions.

- Think back over your life. Have there been any occasions where you have wanted something with all your heart and it happened? List these things.

- Are there any similarities across the instances you recall? Did you take a similar approach? Have a particular mindset? What do you think enabled these things to happen as opposed to anything else you've truly wanted?

- Choose one thing that you'd like to manifest or create in your life. Check back on your Soulful life plan from Chapter 8 if you can't think of anything. Now make a mini-manifestation plan for this thing.

  - Be clear about why you really want it. When you want it. What size you want it in. Be specific.
  - Decide how you will create space for it in your life. What may be blocking it coming to you?
  - How will you be open to the actions you may need to take to get into position for receiving this thing? Remember, you have a part to play too.
  - How can you detach from the 'wanting' and focus on doing what you love right now?
  - How can you bring yourself more into alignment with this desire?

Simple promise

Make this simple promise to yourself now. Remind yourself of this promise throughout your day or write it down where you will see it.

All I desire comes to me with ease and grace.

Simple practices

These simple steps can help you put the ideas in this chapter into practice. Remember, there is power in doing something. Anything. Just one thing. Because the moment you do, you make a conscious change in your life.

Become a clear magnet. Release all doubts, disbelief and feelings of unworthiness about the things you desire in order to increase your pulling power.

Have a bliss circle. Surround yourself with people who believe in you and your dreams, and hold that vision for you too. They amplify your pulling power.

Place an order. Bring focused intention to your life on a monthly, weekly, even daily basis. What do you want to manifest? Remember, the Universe delights in bringing you gifts. But first you must place an order. Be as specific as you can. The more detail you use, the more you fine-tune your ability to attract all you desire.

Start small. Have fun asking for little manifestation miracles. A parking space. An unexpected gift. A green smoothie. A compliment from a stranger. Put the intention out there and see what you receive. It will give you confidence to start asking for bigger things.

Visualise. For bigger dreams, use your visual powers of manifestation. Create a vision board. Play a movie in your mind every night of everything you want as though it was real. Talk to people with enthusiasm about all you desire.

♡

simple meditation

Make Miracles

Get comfortable in your meditation space.

Breathe deeply and feel all tension leave you. Relax.

See yourself coming to centre. Mind, body, emotion and spirit.

Fill your heart with all you dream and desire.

Infuse your hopes with love and positive energy.

Believe you deserve this goodness and more.

Trust your wishes will be answered beautifully, perfectly.

Be patient. Know you do not need to control, you only need to believe.

Allow yourself to receive all the blessings of the Universe.

As it blesses you, you bless it.

Breathe in love. Breathe out love.

Expect magic. Allow miracles. Abundance is yours.

All you desire comes to you with ease and grace.

And so it is.

CHAPTER 10

secret 10: be authentically you

The only person you are destined to become is the person you decide to be.
~ Ralph Waldo Emerson

Being authentic and living your life aligned to your purpose and your deepest values and beliefs is the key to being in Soul flow. This chapter will give you the keys to being authentically you.

Sometimes the things holding us back from being our authentic selves aren't the big, obvious factors that first come to mind. The biggest challenge to becoming my authentic self wasn't losing more than 20kgs in weight. It wasn't leaving my first marriage. It wasn't overcoming depression. It wasn't quitting my job. It wasn't selling up everything for a more simple life. It wasn't even making peace with what other people would think about those things.

My psychic 'coming out' has been the most deeply confronting thing I've done to honour my authentic self.

Looking back, I can see that I've always had heightened awareness and abilities. But when you grow up with them, and you don't know any different, you just assume that everyone else is like you too. That it's the norm. As I moved from childhood to my teenage years, I soon realised that was not the case. I also slowly came to realise that those parts of me weren't really acceptable to other people either.

I've talked already about the extended travel my Mr Mac and I took around Europe. Three glorious months country-hopping together. All the space and expansiveness of new cultures, and new experiences also created space for new awareness to make itself known within me.

That awareness was that I needed to stop hiding and start being loud and proud about all of me – my ability to see into Souls, past lives, futures and all. I returned home from those travels and immediately had my psychic 'coming out'.

It's the most awesome thing I've ever done for myself. It's hard to describe what it feels like when you know you no longer have to hide, and when you finally decide to not give two hoots what people think of you.

It's been interesting to see the effect in my life.

On the one hand, being my authentic self has been so incredibly positive. Yeah, I have a Soul hotline, I love crystals and I talk to angels. But I equally love shopping, adore shoes, keep fit, whip up culinary delights, like nice things and get my hair done. The usual, everyday girl kinda things. And it's that authenticity, my ability to be who I truly am in every part of my life, being uniquely me, that has become my point of difference. My purpose is to make everyday Soulful living normal…hot, not hippy; chic, not complicated; simple, not strange!

The more authentic I am, the more I do what I need to do for other people, the more rewards I receive. The more authentic I am, the more on purpose I can be – inner and outer.

Yet, sometimes, you will find people in your life who aren't comfortable with the 'new' you. Even though it's the 'you' you've always been. Just the one who's decided to stop hiding parts of herself and start being her whole self in every part of her life.

It's usually those who are the most inauthentic who react most strongly to your growing authenticity.

I've had friendships drop off the radar, people 'unfriend' me on Facebook (the social travesty that is!), people choose not to include me in social activities. Did that stuff hurt? Of course it did.

I think each of us has a deep need to be accepted for who we truly are. When other people's actions signal that who you are isn't acceptable, well, you've got a decision to make. The decision is, what hurts more? Remaining tightly closed to your own heart, or shedding everyone and everything who would expect you to?

The truth is, inauthentic people judge, especially when others don't fit into the perfectly defined moulds they need to make themselves feel comfortable. And when you start to live authentically, you shine a light back on the people around you about the parts of their own life where they aren't being true. It becomes uncomfortable for them. *You* may even become uncomfortable for them.

For example, in my old life, no one blinked an eye at the high-flying career girl earning heaps of cash, jetting around the world and being at the top of her game. In fact, some people probably even looked up to that 'me' and wanted what I had. It was okay to be successful working for someone else. But now that I'm self-made and doing what I love in a true, authentic way that is about who I really am, some people seem less okay and even uncomfortable with that.

All I'm saying is you know your truth and it's your Soul right to bring the whole, glorious you to the table. Sometimes to say yes to your own authentic self, you have to release anything that is tethering you. That includes the value you place on other people's opinions of you.

Authenticity is really your Soul truth. And when you start exploring that in your own life, you may be surprised where the journey takes you.

When I decided who I wanted to be and how I wanted to feel, it became clear what I needed to do in my life. I wanted to feel more peaceful. But I realised I was feeling anxious because my mind was cluttered and full. I was feeling overloaded because I was eating foods that weighed me down and took all my energy to digest. I was feeling over stimulated because I was lacking a balance between high impact and restful exercise. I was feeling stressed because I was unconsciously holding my breath during my days. When I started to balance these things, even deeper realisations began to surface.

I felt caged when I wanted to feel free. I felt small when I wanted to feel expansive. I felt limited when I wanted to feel limitless. I felt false when I wanted to feel true. I felt asleep when I wanted to feel awake.

The conscious choice to be authentic and live an authentic life creates change. From such a place of inner peace and knowing, your outer life takes on a great clarity. And you can make even more choices that honour you. You can have long overdue conversations. Choose to leave, move on, release. Decide that saying no sometimes means saying yes to yourself. Focus your time and effort on what and who matters. Lighten up and shine. Make life even more beautiful.

To move forward on path and in Soul flow, you not only need to have an idea of your purpose, an intention to make change, and a commitment to take action, you also need to infuse your entire being and life with the new, authentic, shining you.

The power of authenticity

There is a power in living authentically. Authenticity changes your view of yourself, and of your world. Authenticity is a key to Soul happiness.

But what is authenticity? Well for starters, it's about being fully aware of who you are. Connected to your true essence, which I call your Soul truth. And then it's about acting in alignment with that truth.

You don't have to know your purpose. You don't have to have mastered your lessons. But if you live authentically you automatically set about calibrating your existing self with your Soul-self. You create the space in your life for you to express more of who you truly are. And when you do that, you are on purpose.

So in some ways, authenticity is simply self-empowerment. It's when your thoughts, your words and your deeds align. It's when your actions support your true beliefs. It's the ultimate combination of being and doing.

In fact, so many people yearn for deeper authenticity in their lives. We are starting to make more ethical choices as consumers. We demand more transparency of our leaders. We grow organic food – in essence, authentic food. And yet within ourselves we mistake low self-esteem, low moods, low vitality, even low passion, for symptoms of stress, depression, anxiety or overwhelm. When really, I believe they are signs of Soul sadness. Symptoms of spiritual suppression. All stemming from a lack of authenticity and alignment.

So many of us would do better to say yes to who we truly are, and take a good dose of empowered authenticity. Instead we suppress ourselves and continue to wear masks – both to hide from other people, and to hide from ourselves. It's easier that way. Sometimes it's safer to play small. But it's not better.

When you choose the path of authenticity in your life, you step into your Soul power. And that is immense. By living in your own truth, you send a ripple of truth out into the world. And in doing so you create the space for clarity and knowing of your purpose. It's the space in which Soul happiness shows up from the depths of suppression.

Signs you are suppressing your authentic self

New beginnings are often disguised as painful endings. ~ Lao Tzu

The path of authenticity can be scary, confronting, even painful. I'm not going to lie. It's a challenge.

Most of us would rather wear a mask than bare our Soul. Our fears about not fitting in, not being liked, and not being loved, are the biggest reasons we suppress who we truly are and allow our existing self to become dominant. In our desire to be accepted, we shut down our own truth and suppress our authentic self.

- We say things we don't mean.
- We apologise for who we are.
- We feel like we have to explain ourselves.
- We do things we don't believe.
- We make choices we don't like.
- We accept things we'd rather not.
- We bend ourselves to other people's will.
- We hang on to people we know we shouldn't.
- We dismiss our own needs as pure selfishness.
- We believe we don't deserve good things.

I have done all of these things in my life. And more. I've said and done things that deep down I know are not who I am. I suspect we all have. And we do them mostly for the sake of harmony. We tell ourselves they're only small things. They don't really matter. But to our Soul-self the message is deafening. *You are not worthy. Your needs are not important. Your beliefs don't matter. You are not good enough. You are not lovable.*

And when we tell ourselves those things enough, we end up with not just one mask. We end up with dozens and dozens. One for every circumstance and interaction where we find ourselves pretending to be someone else. And all in a misguided attempt to be liked, loved and accepted. I've been there. I dulled myself down in ways that were comfortable for everyone else, but so destructive to myself. But deep down, I knew I wanted to feel more alive, more joyful and more myself.

The truth is being authentically you in every part of your life takes courage. It takes a willingness to see past the discomfort. It takes an ability to be accepting of all of yourself.

Living authentically in tune with your Soul truth requires a transformation.

But first it requires a decision. Just one. *You are beautiful. You are perfect. You are enough.* That's the decision.

And when you decide that, you are giving yourself permission to be 100 percent comfortable in your own skin. Maybe you don't even know what that feels like. And that's ok. But you will start to feel different. Your vibe will be different. You will feel connected. You will draw opportunities towards yourself that you never felt possible. And you will be increasingly surrounded with similarly true people, who love you for who you really are.

Soul happiness has a habit of cradling you, and looking after you when you say 'Yes' to it.

Claim your Soul power

Living authentically is about knowing it is safe to allow your true power to shine. Your truth to shine. You have to remember, you are the vehicle. Without you, the real you cannot shine. You have a choice in every moment about how you will choose to be.

A belief that is really important to me is the value of all life, and the connectedness of everything. I've already talked about my dietary preferences in this book. They are a way for me to authentically live my beliefs. I prefer the capture and release method for removing insects or spiders from my home. My cats wear collars with bells to alert birds and other animals they are near (my kitten has a habit of wanting to catch butterflies and crickets to play with). I choose not to buy or wear leather clothing and shoes. I support animal shelters. It is important to me that I authentically live my values. It would be untrue of me to say that I love animals and value all life, and then eat meat or wear the hides of animals.

These kinds of personal beliefs and lifestyle choices make you open fodder for others. The key is to stand firm in your beliefs, your choices and who you are, no matter the opinions of others. When you do, you access your deeper power, and with each future authentic choice you become more and more brilliant. You allow the light of your true self to shine even brighter. When you have the courage to live your truth in an authentic, self honouring way, you give others the permission to do the same.

People model what they see. Think of fashion. What is 'in' and 'trendy' is dictated to us every year. Whether it's clothes, homewares, interior design, or even colours. We are told what is acceptable. And more often than not, we follow fashion. It's the next new thing. The next fad. We are simply modelling what we see. In a mass commercial, manufactured way. Usually without a thought to the source of the products we are buying, the conditions, wages, or treatment of the people who make our clothes or the new fruit bowl for our table.

If we want the world to be a different place, it starts with being our authentic selves. Modelling a new way of being that is about individualism and truth, power and choice. Fashion is just another way we conform. I love fashion, don't get me wrong. But I have my own style, and I'm no longer the sort of person I used to be; the one who had to have a new outfit for *every* occasion.

These days I am more thoughtful about how and where I choose to spend my money. Money makes the world go round, as the saying goes, and I am keenly aware that every dollar I spend is like casting a vote for the kind of world I want to live in. Do I want it to be a world that values all people and animals, cherishes the environment, and embraces peace? Yes I do. And every dollar I spend, and every dollar you spend, is like deciding which world you most want to live in.

So you see, you can be authentic in every part of your life, in every breath, in every moment, in every word, in every choice, in every action.

And lots of people won't get it. Which is where you have to make a decision about what is more important to you – being your authentic self in every part of your life; or making decisions that don't resonate with you simply because you worry about what friends, colleagues and others may think.

What's really happening is the more you authentically live your life in sync with your Soul-self, the more you are attuning your energy to your pure self. Your vibration naturally changes. And everything is energy and vibration. When you change, it's inevitable that in parts of your life, vibe 'incompatibility' will develop and people with whom you were once close may fall away. Be your authentic self, and trust me on this, you will invite beautiful new experiences, opportunities, and people into your life. That's Soul power.

The keys to living authentically

To live authentically you are consciously creating space for the true you. Living authentically, embracing your Soul truth and standing in your Soul power are all attainable in your life right now using these four keys.

Be true

Living authentically means allowing yourself to see truth in every part of your life and expressing it. Soul truth comes from your values, your beliefs, your desires.

You may be great at being true to yourself all the time. Doing your own thing in the face of opposition. Standing true to a value when making a key life decision. Walking away from a situation you know doesn't serve you.

Or you may feel wobbly at times, compromising yourself. Eating at a restaurant serving cuisine you don't like because it's a group choice. Putting off an afternoon planning your amazing year because a friend asks you to help them move house. Wearing your hair up because your boyfriend likes it, even though you prefer it down.

Wherever you are at, the fact is, when you start to change your inner self your outer life will respond. And the more awareness you bring to that process, the easier the path becomes.

Think of it like this, companies often have a 'culture'. It's sometimes called corporate culture or company culture. In some places I've worked it's been called 'the way we do things around here'. It often involves a series of catchy statements that communicate the company's values, to which employees are required to adhere. Living authentically is like creating your own company culture. A culture of your own truth. The way you choose to live based on what you value and what you believe.

Be light

Lightness of spirit brings an even greater ability for authenticity to show up in your life simply because of who you choose to be. Lightness of spirit is about being centred and clear, it's about expecting good things in life, and it's about doing what you love and what excites you.

When you are centred and clear, it's easier to love yourself, love your decisions, and let go of the need for others' approval. Free of burden, you become more naturally positive, which leads you to always expect the best. Your positivity becomes a magnet for all you desire, and allows your truest self to be expressed.

Gratitude goes hand-in-hand with lightness of spirit. The more grateful you are, the more love you give and receive. Love is light. And light is expansive and free. That is authenticity.

Be powerful

To be authentic you must take charge of your life. So many of us end up as passive spectators in our own lives, instead of calling the shots.

Taking charge of your life is powerful self-expression. It allows you to let go of anything that isn't for your highest good so you are free to be authentically you.

Being powerful is about believing in yourself enough to have the courage to be uniquely you. It means bringing your truth and your light to every part of your life. Even if it means that standing in your own truth makes others uncomfortable because they are not yet being true to themselves.

Self-full self-love underpins your powerful self-expression. Always allow yourself what you need. Ensuring your needs are met and taking care of yourself are essential self-full practices that allow more of your true self to shine.

Be the path

In the beautifully poignant words of Buddha, you need to become the path. You cannot expect to get where you want to go, or express your authentic Soul truth, if you see it as an end destination. Once more, this is about alignment. Aligning your intention with your action. Your desires with your deeds. Your inner with your outer.

Authenticity is a choice. Decide to be authentically you; decide to live by your values and your ideals; decide to say yes to every part of yourself. Then you'll find you already are everything you wanted to be.

To stay on the path, do two things. Firstly, see that you are already perfect just the way you are. You don't need to strive for ideals that aren't yours to live. And secondly, simplify your life. We allow things to become overcomplicated and over distracted, when all we really need to do is simplify our lives to allow our pure essence to shine.

When you open to your Soul-self, allow the voice of purpose to seek you out, and open your heart to Soul happiness, you start an inner process. Just like when the bud blooms into an exquisite flower. Allow yourself to live your life in the most authentic way you can, and even in those moments along the way when you may question, *What am I doing?*, you will feel the deep anchor of self-knowing keeping you true. Choosing to live authentically both places faith in, and creates space for, the future you.

Simple reflection

In its most simple form, living authentically is about living in tune with your values and your deepest truth. This reflection will guide you to see how you can be more true to yourself.

In a new page of your journal, or on the relevant page in your Soul Happiness companion workbook, consider the following questions.

- Are you being authentically you or are you suppressing your truth? How many of the statements on page 166 ring true for you?

- Do you stand strong in your own power in the world? If not, ask yourself:
    - Am I hiding from who I really am?
    - Who am I hiding from?
    - What am I hiding from?
    - Why am I hiding?

- How can you embody more of the things you truly believe or feel in your life?

- What's one thing – one change, one new approach, one new thought pattern – you can do that will open yourself up to being more authentically you in your life?

- Think about how companies often have a 'company culture' or 'the way we do things around here'. If you were to create your own culture of being true to you, how would you sum it up in one or two sentences?

Simple promise

Make this simple promise to yourself now. Remind yourself of this promise throughout your day or write it down where you will see it.

I honour who I am in my heart, knowing it is safe to be me.

Simple practices

These simple steps can help you put the ideas in this chapter into practice. Remember, there is power in doing something. Anything. Just one thing. Because the moment you do, you make a conscious change in your life.

Be comfortable with you. One of the keys to authenticity is standing in the power of who you are. You do that when you love all of you, including your body. When you are totally comfortable with who you are you allow your true essence to shine.

Be honest. A key habit for authentic living is telling the truth. Admit when you're wrong. Own up to your mistakes. Only speak what is true for you. Only share what your own eyes see as truthful.

Check in. Ask yourself every day "Is there ease, lightness and joy in my life today?" If you can't answer yes become aware of what is blocking you from living authentically.

Do what you say you will. Keep the promises you make and follow through on what you say you will do. Having your words and your deeds in alignment is a key part of being authentic.

Let your values guide you. For one day, or even one hour, practice being authentically you in every part of your life. Only say and do what resonates as your truth. And then increase the period of time for your practice. Notice how you feel when you are being authentically you and when you're not.

Surround yourself with authentic people. It is harder for us to be our true selves when we surround ourselves with inauthentic people. Surround yourself with others who love who you are, rather than what you do or what you have.

.... ❧ ....

Be proactive. Often we surround ourselves with things we may not be ready to deal with, and that suppresses our truth. We procrastinate. So, fix the fridge. Book your dentist check-up. Politely decline that invitation. Do the things you are putting off.

CHAPTER 11

secret 11: grow some more

And the day came when the risk to remain tight in a bud
was more painful than the risk it took to blossom.
~ Anais Nin

The truth about making a Soul connection between your being, your life, and your purpose is that you will be forever changed. Looking back, you will see there were many times where you felt like you were an imposter in your own life. Disconnected from yourself. From your truth. Barely present, barely functioning. And you will be shocked that you were so utterly unaware of such significant misalignment in your life.

You'll start to understand your past in an entirely new light. You'll see photos. You'll recall a situation. You'll have a blinding epiphany with a long awaited insight about a distant moment. And now that you know what it feels like to be connected, what Soul happiness feels like, anything that doesn't resonate with your new being becomes obsolete.

It's not so much that you change. On the one hand you're still you. But on the other hand, you know you *have* changed. It's like you stop being your shadow self and you step into your full Soul power. It's that meeting of the physical and the spiritual that makes expression in your life – of self, of love, of purpose, of joy – effortless.

It's not so much that I've changed. I know I've always been me. And yet right now I feel so much more me than I ever have before. I look back on photos from even a few years ago and I find it hard to connect with the woman I see. She seems Soulless. She feels like a different person to me. She feels, in truth, little more than an existential shell wearing too many masks to see who she truly was.

One of my many masks manifested as adult acne. The bane of my existence since I was in my early 20s. Every year it seemed to get worse and worse. I'm not talking just the odd little pimple here and there. I am talking big, hulking doozies. In clusters. Or under the skin. It was truly horrid. I had such clear beautiful skin as a teenager. And I regretted taking it for granted every night as I lathered on cream after cream. I tried every cleanser, every potion, every treatment I could get my hands on. Nothing worked. So instead I would plaster makeup on and get on with my day. I had a little reprieve for a few years when I used a common three-step solution that is advertised worldwide and even endorsed by celebrities. But eventually even that couldn't keep my skin clear.

It got to the point in my mid-30s where I was so conscious of my skin, it was impacting on my daily life. I would be sitting in high-profile board meetings, nutting out big business decisions, all the while obsessing about whether people were zoning in on the massive zit between my brow or the Vesuvius cluster on my chin.

When I decided to remove all chemicals from my life as a step towards living authentically – including home cleaning products, laundry products, make up, and skin care – it meant giving up that three-step celebrity-endorsed solution. The mental addiction to it overshadowed the actual benefit it was having on my skin anyway.

And then, it was like my skin got one hundred times worse. I persevered with the natural approach, determined not to go back to the harsh chemicals. I tried positive affirmations. Energy healing. Chakra cleansing. Clearing belief systems. All to no avail.

Do you know when my skin started to improve? Naturally. The moment I quit my job and started on my path of purpose. With absolutely zero potions or lotions or expensive salon treatments. It was like all the masks I'd been hiding behind, all the fears I harboured, all the judgements I'd fixated on, just fell away. And within six months so did the acne that I'd lived with, agonised and cried over for more than 15 years.

How? Because, on a Soul level, I stepped away from my shadow self and into my full Soul power. Why? Because I no longer needed to hide who I truly was.

I look back on those years and I look dull and flat in photos. I don't say that with self-judgement, I'm simply observing the fact that my light, my glow, my spirit were completely shut down. Hidden.

Today I feel like I glow. And what's different? I've integrated my spiritual self and my physical self, I've aligned my inner and my outer, and I'm living with purpose. I'm in Soul flow.

Now, it's like I have a powerful aura of who I am. I know my own truth and I know my purpose. And that literally radiates. People comment on my photos saying I look like I'm 'glowing' or I look 'radiant' or I look 'angelic'.

The only thing that's changed is I've said yes to my spirit and been courageous enough to leave my shadow life and step into my light. It's my light that people can see now.

And it's your light that is calling you too. It's calling you to leave your shadow life behind. To allow your masks to crumble. To step into your full potential. To become whole.

The point of this chapter is to help you understand that the journey of the Soul is limitless, and to give you the keys you need to ensure the limitless growth of your Soul in this lifetime.

The anatomy of change

The secret of change is to focus all of your energy not on fighting the old, but on building the new. ~ Socrates

If you commit to the programme of discovery in this book – even if you just dabble here and there – and start to ask some deeper questions about the truth of yourself and your very reason for being here, you are going to start to change. To grow, you must change. Perhaps emerge is a better word. Unfurl. Blossom. Light-up. Awaken. Whatever word resonates for you, it still requires change. And that's ok. In fact, anything that allows you to step closer to your Soul truth, and your Soul-self is in a word, wonderful.

Throughout this book I provide suggestions that, if you choose to, require you to change a belief or a habit. By reading it, you will know what you could do. But it's likely there will be a gap between knowing what to do, and choosing to do it.

It's not often we get something for nothing, at least that's what my parents used to say to me when I was growing up. Growing means changing. Into the person you are meant to be. Destined to be. So, I encourage you to address the ways you may be limiting positive change in your life now.

Change means doing something. Change requires you to choose to do something. Change requires your focus, your time, your determination and action. Change requires your intention, but it doesn't manifest until you also focus your attention. Change requires energy.

Change means giving up something. When we focus on change we tend to think of what we will lose. It strikes me that we use the language of loss all too frequently. *I need to lose weight. My relationship ended. I lost my job.* How about looking at it another way. Focus on what you will gain. Lose weight; gain lightness. End a relationship; open yourself to a more fulfilling one. Lose a job; create an opportunity for something you are passionate about. Change usually requires giving up something you want, for something you want more.

Change is easier than you think. Mostly we shun change. It's uncomfortable and difficult. Sometimes it even hurts. Change puts us right outside our comfort zone.

While it might not start off easy, pretty soon change becomes our new comfort zone. Think about something in your life that you've changed. Perhaps you started jogging rather than walking for your exercise. Your muscles certainly protested the difference, your lungs cried out in protest too, and your mind told you you couldn't possibly go one step further. But eventually, with focus, time and determination, you found yourself effortlessly jogging further than you ever thought you could. Even starting a new job – you don't know the people, you don't know where the stationery cupboard is, and you have to get used to new systems and processes. But pretty soon it will feel like you've always been there. Part of the furniture, as they say.

Change requires a deep desire for something better. To shift from knowing to doing you need a goal; an inspiring dream that will shine for you. You have to know what you're working towards. Why you're doing it. What you really want for yourself. When you feel yourself wavering, this is that dream that will keep going and remind you why you're worth it.

Change needs space. The most important thing you can do is be open, and create the space in your life to support yourself and your needs. Any programme of change requires time. And space. Give yourself both. Because you need to change the way you think before you can be.

Know that when you choose to be different, you automatically start an internal recalibration at the deepest level. As part of that recalibration you need to create space for the new you, and it is inevitable that anything that needs clearing or that doesn't serve your highest good will come up. This is so you can have awareness of it and let it go.

Your Soul-self is the same as anything in your life. To have room for the new, you have to let go of the old.

Change means getting off track. Getting off track is predictably inevitable. It's going to happen at some point. With greater frequency for some of us than others. In my experience the closer you journey inward, the more you connect with your Soul, the more natural it seems you will get off track but the easier it is to regain perspective and balance.

We've all had those shadowy moments of self-doubt, and questioning and worry. For me they tend to come with frequency when I'm right on the cusp of something truly magnificent. And I also know that they're essential to my growth. It's where our insight, learning and inner wisdom comes from. The key is to accept and choose how to be in each moment, rather than obsess and resist.

Those negative, shadowy feelings have a source. And once we see that we are both the cause and effect, we expand our awareness of ourselves and of life. We are the cause because, knowingly or unknowingly, we focus on pleasing others before honouring ourselves, on believing that what others think makes a true difference in our life, and on moulding and squashing ourselves into someone else's view of how we should be. And all because we want to feel worthy of being loved.

There's just one thing to remember. Getting off track is essential for growth.

Change means being comfortable with the uncomfortable. A key challenge is being comfortable with feeling uncomfortable. What you most resist is what you most need. It is those things that are going to stretch and grow and challenge you and ultimately create the space for your dream life to fill. I treat being uncomfortable as I sign I am on the right path. In fact, the greater my resistance, the louder my fear, the more I know my heart is pointing me in the direction of something of great importance.

Let's be clear though. Being uncomfortable is not a negative thing. It's not about feeling like rubbish or being utterly miserable or tying yourself up in knots of anxiety. I'm talking about the kind of uncomfortable where you have butterflies in your stomach, you catch your breath or you feel your pulse quicken. It's uncomfortable excitement topped with a drizzle of resistance.

I've discovered that, usually, when things feel difficult in my outer life, it's because there is equilibrium to be reached. Like this book. It's taken me more than a year, on and off, to write. I've been so close so many times to finishing. And then something happens. Resistance. But it happens because the book needs something that hasn't quite come to my awareness yet. And so I would set it aside. Waiting until the resistance passed and I could continue writing. I've learnt there's always a reason for 'go slows' in my life. Always. I say love that resistance. It's making room for an even better outcome.

The principles of Soul growth

I have said many times before in this book, and I will repeat it again now: the Soul only presents you with what you are ready for. Everything in your life happens in just the right way and at exactly the right time.

It's such an important idea to grasp. Because the ultimate state of being for Soul growth is the one in which you are 100 per cent attuned to your Soul essence, your purpose and your reasons for being here. Your highest, truest self can only come to the party if the you that is here right now on this earthly ride, is open to the love and joy within you and the potential of all that you are.

You have freewill. You may choose to do nothing. Change nothing. That choice is yours.

But if you choose to allow your Soul-self to lead, if you choose to live through your heart and follow your bliss, magic will happen.

Yes, you will be challenged. But you will be transformed. Yes, you may feel worry still. But you will see the truth of your life. Yes, you may feel overwhelmed. But it will be your own light that guides you.

Never underestimated how much you are loved. Say "Yes" to your spirit and marvel at how your Soul-self gently guides and coaxes you forward. Every step moves you closer to your true purpose. And with every step you receive more. Dreams are answered. Wishes fulfilled. Gifts bestowed. Desires manifested. Hearts start bursting with pure love and happiness. Become the path and Soul happiness will come to greet you.

Do I think I've attained my true purpose? I know I haven't. I know I'm on path and I'm living with purpose. But I know there's more to come. Do I even know what my true purpose looks like? Kind of. But I know I can only see the stepping stones that are right in front of my nose. I know they are leading me somewhere that, right now, I can't quite imagine.

And with my belief that everything happens in the perfect time, and my knowing that I've got to hold up my end of things 'down here', I am committed to moving forward. I'm committed to allowing my truest self to grow at whatever rate it wants to. I know I will go deeper. I will learn. And then I will grow some more. I know ultimately I am in charge. And I choose to live my life as authentically as I can in each moment, while also following my own principles for growth.

I know along the way I will touch lives, inspire belief, heal with love, and help others step into their own power and beauty. And it excites me. And I know the inner reflects the outer. All love, joy and beauty shared from a place of truth and purpose, will return to me in abundance and with prosperity. Such is Soul happiness.

There are four key principles of Soul growth. They work regardless of where you are on your path. They work regardless of whether you are aware of your lessons and purpose or not. Following these principles creates an order in your life for growth and development. They are designed to allow you to create the space for the limitless you. They are simple to follow and easy to implement in your life.

Energy + Environment

The first principle of Soul growth is Energy + Environment. New flowers do not survive in a weed-choked garden bed. Nor will your blossoming Soul have the space it needs to grow in stagnant energy and a cluttered environment. To live a life of purpose and to open yourself to the cycle of stepping ever closer to who you truly are, you need to prepare yourself and your environment. This is about having both the space and the environment to cultivate your truest potential. This is the foundation that supports you.

- **Create order.** I've talked a lot about order in this book. I think it's my favourite concept. And that's because whether we're talking about spiritual notions, or talking about something in the here and now, order is so important for the smooth flow in any part of your life. The space around you needs room for energy to flow with ease. My home environment always feels lighter and brighter, and so do I, when I've had a good spring clean and declutter. Choose to detach from anything – and anyone – that no longer uplifts you or serves your highest good. Replace heaviness in your home and your heart with loving, peaceful energy. Have a lightness and simplicity to your life, and you will be freer to step easily in whatever direction you choose.

- **Detoxify.** It is not just the spaces in which we live that need clearing. The inner clutter we accumulate within ourselves can weigh us down and hold us back too. It is not until I released toxins, foods, thoughts, hurts, beliefs and more from my life that I realised how much my physical, mental and emotional self was stifling my spirit. Clear your energy and commit to a regular and conscious cycle of healing on every level of your being to create space for your true self to expand.

- **Allow time.** You cannot force anything in life. There is a natural order. Not just to nature, but to your own Soul growth too. Trying to force anything to happen at a rate faster or slower than it naturally intends to causes unnecessary stress. You may want all the answers to your deepest questions right now – who you are, what your purpose is, what you need to do – but the truth is, no one has the answers but you. Growth happens in its own time. Create the space, allow the time, and everything you need will come to you perfectly and with ease.

- **Trust.** There will come a point when you will need to take a leap of faith and step into the unknown. Perhaps it's already happened for you. And it will keep happening, because at times stepping into the unknown is the greatest test of our ability to believe in ourselves and our potential. While the path may not always be clear to your physical eyes and your thinking self, your wisest self knows exactly where you are going. You are being guided every step of the way. The only person you have to trust is yourself. And sometimes, as I've discovered, the biggest risks and the scariest decisions are the ones that finally set you free.

Clarity + Connection

The second principle of Soul growth is Clarity + Connection. This is about attitude, intent, perspective, truth. It is seeing clearly by having a connection to yourself and your deepest truth. It's the difference between living caged, and finally stepping into the light. Like finally perceiving the beauty of the day and the vastness of the stars. It's about awareness of your full potential. By doing so you are automatically empowered to make decisions and take steps that honour your truth. Your potential in this time and place is limitless. And once you start the journey you find a place of pure joy and contentment.

- **Live from truth.** Replace your deep self-limiting programmes with the truth in your heart. You are expansive. Get out of whatever box you've been stuffed in; that is not your truth. Rather it's the truth of you as determined by others. Release those constraints and raise your awareness of your own self instead. Explore your shadow self, embrace it, love it for all it can teach you. For that is how you truly know yourself and become able to express more of who you authentically are. Accept that you already know your own truth, know who you are and know what you are here to give.

- **Live with intent.** Perhaps the single most important thing you can do for your spiritual path is to live with intent. The intention you have for yourself, your life, and all you desire will be returned to you. Intention brings clarity and connection to your truth. And when you're clear about what you want, you are more likely to receive it. The attitude you have and the choices you make are the heart of your self-expression.

- **Live with grace.** When you see a blessing in every moment, you go further than seeing the truth of your life. You see the truth of *all* life. Every situation or struggle embodies both a gift and a challenge. There is always a balance and a blessing in every moment. And when you take the time to feel gratitude for all the goodness in your life – the simple, the everyday, and the profound – you grant yourself the beauty of peace and contentment.

- **Believe.** Have an innate sense of self-worth and self-belief. You are special. It's as simple as that. Be unshakable and independent even in the face of criticism and judgement. Make your own rules. Be daring and do what you know is right for you. Harness your full creative power. Combine intention and action to manifest all you desire. You are powerful. You are always safe. Self-belief and self-love create enduring clarity and connection with your truth.

Purpose + Practice

The third principle of Soul growth is Purpose + Practice. If you feel a higher calling, you have a higher calling. Honour your spirit with an answer. And honour your spirit with the practice that supports that answer. Accept that all new beginnings start with you and know that the more on path and purpose you are, the deeper bliss you will feel. We are here to gain wisdom to reach our highest potential. Even in life we seek to go higher, do better, be more. The natural urge to grow is an inherent part of our Soul-self. Usually we experience considerable inner growth before it starts to reflect in the outer. Your job is to allow natural Soul growth and flex your spiritual fitness, all the while being gentle on yourself. Remember, inner transformation cannot be seen as it occurs.

- **Embrace lessons.** Every stepping stone on our path is leading to the highest expression of ourselves and our intention for this life. At each point we are presented with opportunities to master our lessons, particularly those relating to our emergence as the most fully realised aspect of ourselves. Life lessons are about growth, so in seeking to serve ourselves and others, we must also learn. Embrace life's lessons, remember there is a blessing always, and know it is all connected to your higher purpose.

- **Give with love.** Ultimately each of us is here to be of service to ourselves and to others. That is our higher calling. And we do that through love. The more you commit to merging love and service, the more space you create for your true purpose to awaken.

- **Train yourself.** Like anything you are seeking to expand in life – knowledge, fitness, experience, prosperity – Soulful living takes practice. It takes training. Practice creates potency. Having a spiritual practice creates space for spiritual growth and development. A spiritual practice is about simply coming back to centre; returning to your place of inner zen and reflection every day. When you exercise your Soul daily, you naturally find your wellbeing and your inner strength. It's this balance that is vital for each forward step on your path and purpose. Think of a daily spiritual practice as maintenance, whereas monthly and yearly practices take you deeper. See suggestions for spiritual practices at the end of this chapter.

Essence + Oneness

The fourth principle of Soul growth is Essence + Oneness. In some ways this principle is the hardest to articulate. It is about having a deep reverence for all. It's about opening your mind and your heart to a deeper understanding of yourself and a more expansive view of your world. It's about consciously choosing to release your ego-self and step more into your Soul-self and all that is, every single day. It's about the divine connection within yourself, with others, with the planet. It's about knowing you are everything, living from your heart, and choosing to flow with love and acceptance, peace and joy. It's about being your truest essence. Love.

- **Release illusion.** Throughout this book I've shared much about the layers of illusion we become tightly bound in. Layer upon layer of illusion. More often by circumstance than choice. But we become wrapped so tightly in illusion that we see ourselves as separate from our Soul-selves, and it becomes fear that propels us forward and suffering that consumes us. There is no separation. Of anything. The merest thought triggers a chain reaction of epic proportions. It creates an emotion. It stifles or expands our energy. It sends ripples into the infinite field. And like a boomerang, it will be returned in a form that fits the original intention. Everything is connected. You are one with the all.

- **Know divinity.** Every moment is a divine creation. I have experienced the (extra)ordinary divine, as I'm sure you have. The freshness and freedom of wind in your hair. The magical sunset that seems to speak to your Soul. The delicate splendour of new life. Yet too often we are too hurried to see them unfolding in all their beauty before our eyes. We think that God or a higher power is beyond our reach. Separate. Holy. Other. But divinity is every day. Before you. Within you. Around you. The true experience of divinity comes from our ability to experience oneness, to be present, to feel love in every single, simple, beautiful moment.

- **Love.** You're reading this book, so chances are you love love. The feeling of it. The form of it. You probably want more of it too. Love is the secret. The key. The one thing above all else that stirs Soulful living, that says yes to your spirit, that creates room for your purpose to find you. Living from love is the essence of Soul happiness. The key is to decide 'to love'. To have love as both the intent and the action. Decide to love your body. Decide to love your mind. Decide to love your work. Decide to love your feelings. Decide to love others. Decide to love all. And the decision to love gives you permission to nourish yourself well with nutrition and exercise, feed your mind with learning, bring excitement and enthusiasm to your work, and to respect and honour how you feel. The decision to love in your life will transform your world. When you decide to love you naturally align your inner and outer self. Love is your true state of being.

Let your intuition be your guide

Being authentic and allowing yourself to grow and expand is about trusting your deepest self and your intuition. This becomes more important the more on purpose you become.

No matter where you are in your life, your intuition is vital. In fact, I believe unlocking it at the deepest levels is the fourth aspect of our purpose. I call it our 'Divine Purpose'. My next book, *Intuitive Happiness*, is dedicated to guiding you to fully awaken your intuition as the primary guiding tool in your life, and most certainly for aligning to and progressing with your Soul purpose.

Your intuition is your inner voice. I like to call this inner knowing – or intuition or higher guidance – the voice of your heart. It is the voice that comes from a place of love and respect and is always working for your highest good. We have other voices of course. The ones that are negative and horrible about other people, and ourselves. In your life, choose to give your power to the voice of your heart rather than the voice of your ego in your head. When you decide to listen to and follow the voice of your heart, you choose a path of grace and life literally flows.

Perhaps your intuitive, sixth sensory gifts are fully awakened. If not, you need to realise that you are already more intuitive than you realise. It's not just a weird coincidence that you feel you know what your baby wants, and how to calm her before she can even talk. Or that you are thinking of someone and then you randomly bump into them or receive a phone call, email or message out of the blue. Or that you know how your friend is really feeling inside, even though she tells you "I'm fine" Or that you purchase a home fire extinguisher the day before a fry pan full of oil catches fire on your stove. It is the little voice of your heart quietly guiding you. And the more you listen, the louder it will become.

You already contain within you everything you need to realise your Soul purpose. Your heart and intuition, your spirit, know what you are to become. They have left the trail of crumbs in your life. When you tune fully into your intuition – which you do through balancing mind, body, emotion, spirit – you create the space to allow yourself to see with clarity, connect the dots, live with purpose and follow your bliss.

Respond to every call that excites your spirit

Conscious evolution is exactly what your Soul is doing here on earth. It is a deceptively simple cycle of expansion in which you step forward, soak up learning and awareness, pause to reflect and see how far you've come… and then step forward to go deeper still.

That is your purpose. And the more you authentically live in alignment with who you really are, the more you will be guided to the next stepping stone or next level in your outer purpose. The key is to always be true to yourself, and do what excites and inspires you. The secret is to take action.

There is not simply one level of expansion or growth, but many. This is just the start. You will grow, you will change, you will see things, do things, achieve things, and you will give, receive and experience more than you can comprehend.

You only need to start small. Usually it's about doing simple things, small things. These simple and small things lead you to more. You will be guided where you need to go. Always.

Investing in yourself with awareness, love, time, and belief is the best investment you will ever make. It will help you live authentically and with a clarity of truth and purpose.

On the path of purpose and spirit, there is only one thing to remember.

In the words of Rumi, respond to every call that excites your spirit. When you do that, you will always be honouring your truest self. And there is no greater foundation for Soul happiness.

Simple reflection

The nature of the Soul is to learn, grow and expand. It is a constant theme of expansion in our lives, ensuring that with every cycle we become a lighter, brighter version of ourselves, more connected to our Soul-self and more able to be on path and on purpose. This reflection is designed to give you the insights for how you can create the space and awareness for Soul growth in your life.

- As always, turn to a new page in your journal, or the relevant page in your Soul Happiness companion workbook.

- At what points in your life do you feel like you've been off-track? What did those moments teach you? How did you grow from them?

- Have you experienced feelings of inner resistance, fear or worry at times in your life when you've been on the cusp of something amazing? What did those moments teach you? How did you grow from them?

- If you look back on the last 10 years of your life from the perspective of Soul growth, what do you see? Have you changed? What have you learnt? Have you stepped closer to who you truly are? Do you shine more brightly?

- Consider the Principles of Soul Growth starting on page 181. Which principles most resonate with you? Which most challenge you? Which most intrigue you? Which can you apply to your life more?

- Take a fresh page in your journal and divide it into four squares, one each for: Energy + Environment, Clarity + Connection, Purpose + Practice, and Essence + Oneness. Make a commitment to yourself in each area and list a step (or steps) you can take to achieve that. Read the simple practices at the end of this chapter for ideas too. This is like your Soul Growth plan. Revisit it annually, or as frequently as you want to.

Simple promise

Make this simple promise to yourself now. Remind yourself of this promise throughout your day or write it down where you will see it.

I give myself permission to step into the full power of my Soul.

Simple practices

The practices below will build on the practices noted in the Principles of Soul Growth in this chapter. They particularly relate to building your spiritual fitness. Remember, there is power in doing something. Anything. Just one thing. Because the moment you do, you make a conscious change in your life.

Commit to a practice. To fully embrace Soul growth, commit to a daily, weekly or monthly practice. Your daily practice could include things that allow you to keep balanced and centred, like a breathing meditation, yoga, tai chi, journaling or visualisation. Your weekly or monthly practice could include things that bring you a deeper Soul connection, like longer guided meditations, receiving healings, joining a meditation group, going to church, walking in nature, taking a spiritual class or course, or doing something for others like volunteering. Spend time designing your ideal Soul growth practice.

Find a teacher. When the time feels right for you, find a teacher, guide or mentor who can help you with your Soul growth and development. When the student is ready the teacher appears, so have faith that you will be drawn to the perfect guide.

Find your 'soulies'. Soulies is a term my friend Charlotte uses for connections at a Soul level. Soulies are your Soul family. When you keep the company of like-minded people who are on the same vibe as you, it is easier to allow Soul growth. When we feel comfortable, it is easier to be ourselves, and when we are ourselves our goals are easier to achieve.

Journal. Journaling is the perfect practice for allowing all the thoughts, intentions, expectations, dreams and wishes you have to come to the surface. Journaling allows you to access your stream of consciousness and helps you connect more with your intuition and deepest truths. Journal in the morning upon waking for the best results.

Love your intuition. Accessing your intuition is one of the best ways to tune into your truth and guidance. Your intuition will connect you to your Soul code, help you stay in Soul flow, and guide your Soul growth. Learn to pay attention to how you feel, and trust it. That's your intuition talking.

Meditate. Make time in your day, every day, to quietly be with yourself and pray or meditate. Even meditating just twenty minutes a day, focusing on your breathing and clearing you mind, will help you feel more relaxed, centred and connected to your truth. When we sit in silence we often gain insights about our next steps. Remember to record in your journal any insights you receive through meditation.

Take Soul time. Design a personal retreat; an annual Soul stay-cation. Make it more frequently if you wish. Take a day, a weekend, a week, and spend time with yourself in solitude. Use it to reflect on the year that has been, to get back in sync, to check in on your plans and create new ones. Read, write, connect. And return feeling happy, refreshed, renewed and with clarity in your heart and your head.

♡

simple meditation

Soul Connection

Get comfortable in your meditation space.

Breathe in through your nose and out through your mouth.

Breathe deeply. Let go.

Know it is time to awaken to you.

Love surrounds and protects you.

Light floods your being with sacred peace and divine love.

Breathe in the light. Become light. Be light.

Connect with your Soul-self. Your shining essence.

Know there is no separation. Only unity. Only love.

Step purposely into the full power of you. Expand. Flourish.

Feel the soft strength, the graceful power of being one.

Claim your Soul right. Embrace your highest truth.

Know it is safe to express the divinity within you.

All you have to do is be.

You are powerful. You are whole. You are one.

Self-fully. Soulfully. Completely.

And so it is

to end

Your Soul whispers, I believe in you. You are beautiful. You are talented. You are special. You are perfect. You can do this. Just believe in you too. Now is your time.

My heart's desire is that in these pages you will find yourself. Your deepest connection with your own truth. The answers to the questions you've always believed answerless. The keys to living the life you really want to live. The power to live your purpose.

Everyone already knows their purpose. They've always known, on some level of their being. And when people say they don't know, or they can't find it, or they don't know where to start, what they are really doing is denying themselves permission to be who they are.

When we are searching for our purpose, what we're really looking for is the opportunity to express our truest self. At a deep level we want to be authentic and live authentically. We want to be happy and experience happiness. We want to love, share love and be loved. Yet there is no one thing, or activity or magic pill that will make you feel happy or be authentic. You have to choose to be happy. Be authentic. Be love. And when you do, all the things, activities, experiences, people that match that feeling will be magnetised to you and start filling your life.

This book guides you not so much on an inner journey, but an inner awakening. The destination is you.

In its pages lie all the secrets to connecting to your Soul-self. It shows you how to unlock your Soul code. Simple insights and tools allow you to access a deeper understanding of who you are, what you are here to learn, and how you can help others. It teaches you that purpose is more expansive than just what you 'do' in the world. It shows you how to effortlessly attain Soul flow. It guides you to align your inner and outer self, your inner and outer worlds, and your inner and outer purpose as the key. And it gives you the practical and spiritual tools to anchor your purpose in your life, manifest your dreams, and allow your Soul to expand.

Ultimately, it shows you the secrets of Soul happiness. It shows you how to be blissfully happy for life by loving yourself, honouring the truth of who are, and authentically living your purpose.

Now sweet Soul, it is your turn. See the beauty of you, the gifts you were born with and the potential of all that you are. Know you have the power to create a powerful flow of radiance and bliss within your life, which touches the lives of others and raises the happiness vibration of humanity.

All you have to do is focus on your feelings. They are the hotline to your Soul. How you want to feel is who you want to be. And who you want to be is who you really are.

Hear the quiet whispers of your heart. Say yes to your spirit. Follow the trail of breadcrumbs and meet yourself anew. Like a friend, long-lost. Remember who you are. Remember you are the key to all the happiness you desire, all the love you yearn for, all the peace you crave, all the fulfilment you need. You, beautiful, are the key to your dreams.

Be who you truly are. Live authentically. Trust your knowing. Create your beautiful life. Step into your full power. Self-fully. Soulfully. Completely. Then, as Buddha says, joy will follow you like a shadow and never leave you. This is Soul Happiness.

11 simple promises

If you do nothing else, decide to make and then keep these simple promises to yourself.

Happiness Is Your Right
I am worthy of blissful, lifelong happiness.

The Soul's Natural Order
I open my heart to receive my highest guidance for my purpose in this life.

Lessons Have Purpose
I am open to seeing the gift in every lesson.

Truth Lives In Your Heart
I see my truth and honour how I feel. Always.

Gifts Are For Sharing
I shine my light and allow my inner and outer worlds to align.

You Are The Path
I see my life with loving eyes and create the space for my Soul to expand.

Say Yes To Your Soul
My purpose is what I know to be true for me.

Create Your Reality
I take action to create my beautiful life.

Manifest Your Dreams
All I desire comes to me with ease and grace.

Be Authentically You
I honour who I am in my heart, knowing it is safe to be me.

Grow Some More
I give myself permission to step into the full power of my Soul.

glossary of terms

Life path: The freewill you have to live a life of your choosing.

Soul: The eternal, permanent part of us that incarnates into a physical body. It is the essence of who we are.

Soul challenges: The lessons you are mastering to help with Soul growth.

Soul character: The innate qualities, passions and gifts you have to share. Sometimes referred to as spirit.

Soul code: The blueprint containing the unique suite of Soul assets you bring into each incarnation.

Soul flow: The state of ease and grace that occurs when life choices are in alignment with Soul purpose.

Soul happiness: The lifelong, enduring state of happiness. Bliss.

Soul path: The trail that connects you to your truth and Soul purpose.

Soul purpose: Your reason for being in this lifetime, comprising inner purpose, outer purpose, shared purpose and divine purpose.

Soul sadness: A disconnection from your Soul caused by suppression of who you are.

Soul values: The inherent values and beliefs you have. Guiding principles for life.

the trinity of soul happiness

You already have your unique Soul code – the expression of who you are in this life time. It's up to you to be in tune with that. The more in tune you are, the happier you will be. It can be no other way.

Connecting to your true self is simply a remembering. Sometimes remembering takes time, space and know-how.

That's where the books in the Happiness of the Soul series come in. Each is designed to give you simple tools and awareness to bring you closer to Soul happiness.

Balance your life

Beyond Happiness: The 12 Principles of Enduring Bliss is the first book in the Happiness of the Soul series. It provides you with the philosophy and the foundation principles of enduring bliss. Through it I show you how to balance your life, and how to know, trust, love and honour yourself in every way by realising the beauty and connectedness of your complete self. The balance of every part of you – mind, body, emotion and Soul – is essential if you are to create the space for Soul happiness.

Live your purpose

This book, *Soul Happiness: The 11 Secrets of Living with Purpose* is the second book in the series. Through it I show you how to authentically live your Soul purpose. In this book you will discover your unique gifts and talents and the four aspects of your purpose for this life. Then you will discover how to blend it all into being by manifesting a life with purpose and living the life of your dreams. Soul Happiness is all about harmonising your dreams and your purpose for the deepest level of happiness.

Unlock your intuition

Intuitive Happiness is the third book in the series. Due for release in 2014, this book will show you how to connect to and trust your highest realms of spiritual guidance, and reclaim your own inner wisdom. This Soul connection is the hidden key in Soul happiness.

ABOUT THE AUTHOR

Marnie McDermott is an award-winning author, heart-fuelled lifestyle coach and host of MarnieTV. Think of her as your crystal-toting, fashion-loving, spiritually-savvy soul sister, giving you the tools, tips and super-charged strategies to live your happiest life.

As the founder of **www.marniemcdermott.com**, Marnie has worked with women from all corners of the globe to create their own version of wholehearted bliss. Her work incorporates powerful tools and programmes focused on spirit-centred living, happiness, life purpose, meditation, abundance, order and harmony, home, relationships, health and wellbeing, and more. Marnie is the go-to girl for soulful living made simple, and her books are hailed as the perfect blend of modern wisdom and practical know-how.

www.ingramcontent.com/pod-product-compliance
Lightning Source LLC
Chambersburg PA
CBHW060236050426
42448CB00009B/1459